# Exploring the Role of Women in the Church

A journey of discovery that demands a response

Richard Burgess

*Exploring the Role of Women in the Church*
Copyright © 2022 by Richard Burgess
Published by Red Oak Publishing, 113 Grosvenor Road, Kennington, Ashford, Kent, UK, TN24 9PN.
Cover design: Debbie Burgess
ISBN: 9798840451724

All rights reserved. No part of this publication may be reproduced, stored in a retrieval system, or transmitted in any form or by any means, electronic, mechanical, photocopy, recording, or otherwise, without the written prior permission of the publisher, except as provided for by copyright law.

Unless otherwise noted all Scripture quotations are taken from The Christian Standard Bible. Copyright © 2017 by Holman Bible Publishers. Used by permission. Christian Standard Bible®, and CSB® are federally registered trademarks of Holman Bible Publishers, all rights reserved.

Scripture quotations marked CEB are from the COMMON ENGLISH BIBLE®. Copyright © 2011 COMMON ENGLISH BIBLE. All rights reserved. Used by permission. (www.CommonEnglishBible.com).

Scripture quotations marked ESV are from the ESV® Bible (The Holy Bible, English Standard Version®), Copyright © 2001 by Crossway, a publishing ministry of Good News Publishers. Used by permission. All rights reserved.

Scripture quotations marked MSG are taken from THE MESSAGE, Copyright © 1993, 2002, 2018 by Eugene H. Peterson. Used by permission of NavPress, represented by Tyndale House Publishers. All rights reserved.

Scripture quotations marked NASB are taken from the (NASB®) New American Standard Bible®, Copyright © 1960, 1971, 1977, 1995, 2020 by The Lockman Foundation. Used by permission. All rights reserved. www.lockman.org

Scripture quotations marked (NIV) are taken from the Holy Bible, New International Version®, NIV®. Copyright © 1973, 1978, 1984, 2011 by Biblica, Inc.™ Used by permission of Zondervan. All rights reserved worldwide. www.zondervan.com The "NIV" and "New International Version" are trademarks registered in the United States Patent and Trademark Office by Biblica, Inc.™

Scripture quotations marked NLT are taken from the Holy Bible, New Living Translation, Copyright © 1996, 2004, 2015 by Tyndale House Foundation. Used by permission of Tyndale House Publishers, Inc., Carol Stream, Illinois 60188. All rights reserved.

I dedicate this book to my wife Pam, and our three children, Tim, Lisa and Debbie who have encouraged and provoked me on the journey.
And to all those who have encouraged, equipped, and enabled me in the ministry over the years.

"On the day that God created man, he made him in the likeness of God; he created them male and female. When they were created, he blessed them and called them mankind."

Genesis 5:1,2 (CSB)

# CONTENTS

Introduction...1

1. Exploring the Big Question...6

2. Exploring the Role of Women in the Old Testament...20

3. Exploring the Role of Women in the New Testament...30

4. Exploring God's Original Intention...39

5. Exploring the Nature of the New Testament Church...48

6. Exploring the Problem Passages...60

7. Exploring Eldership...98

8. Exploring Church History...108

9. Final Thoughts...131

Bibliography...136

# INTRODUCTION

I love questions. Life is full of them, and they are designed to be explored.

What can and what can't women do in the church is a big one. Can they teach, preach, or be an elder or senior leader? The question is one that is well worth exploring. Though a lot has been written in books, papers, and articles over recent years, the question remains unresolved for many.

This book began as my attempt at exploring the subject in greater depth—a project that started a few years ago and increased in earnestness the more I read and studied. If my journey, studies and reflections are of any help to others, whether individuals, couples, or churches, then another book on the subject will have been worthwhile.

Throughout the process, I have read across the spectrum, from the academic to the popular. I have also spent time discussing the subject with others. Throughout, I have desired to rightly divide, understand, and interpret the scriptures, wanting to be clear in my mind about what they have to say. Having done that, I have been encouraged to make it available to others who may be wrestling with the subject.

Though this is by no means an attempt at a full exploration, examining every nuance of possible interpretation—and believe me, there are many—what I write, I do so having sought to read, understand, and get a handle on the subject at some reasonable depth.

## *Words/terminology*

Before we get into it, I need to say something about words or terminology. Words can mean different things to different people. Americans play football, and so do the English, but they are not the same thing, and neither are the rules. Sometimes I'm asked if I'm a particular type of Christian—reformed, evangelical, confessional, charismatic, etc. Before I answer, I find it helpful to discover what the person asking means or understands by those terms, as that gives shape and purpose to both the question and the answer.

Words are containers and give shape to ideas, but to quote Kipling, they are also "the most powerful drug used by mankind." If that is the case, then they can be intoxicating. Jean-Paul Sartre went further and described them as "loaded pistols," which means they have the power to wound, maim or destroy—powerful things words. The old proverb stands true, "Death and life are in the power of the tongue" (Prov 18:21), and, we might add, "the written word." What we mean by them and how we use them, is vitally important.

For a long time, it was thought that language has no impact on the way we think, but modern research has shown otherwise. Lera Boroditsky, a cognitive scientist and professor in the fields of language and cognition, states, "People who speak different languages do indeed think differently and that even flukes of grammar can profoundly affect the way we see the world… appreciating its role in constructing our mental lives brings us one step closer to understanding the nature of humanity."[1] The language we use in this debate, as at all times, is important. With it, we are shaping thoughts and actions, creating cultures. Unfortunately, some of the rhetoric, as we will see, has shaped and polarized the debate, forming a culture, or cultures, that are not healthy and should not be the norm.

The terms, complementarian and egalitarian, are the usual reference points in the debate, though both are broad camps with a wide variety of understanding as to what they mean or encompass. For the sake of this book, I have taken a general definition of both.

**Complementarians** believe that men and women are equal in value and person-hood before God but are created to fulfil different "roles" in marriage, the family, and the church. At one time, this would have included society as well, but with the increasing involvement of women in what once would have been a man's world, from the shop floor to business, from politics to the armed forces, from driving lorries to piloting planes, etc. it is no longer the case. The argument on that one was lost and/or adapted some years ago, though there are still some who believe this should still be the case in some areas of society today.

Complementarianism means in practice that men are those who are called and equipped to lead (make decisions), and women are called to subordinate themselves to male leadership—to submit and follow. Men are also responsible before God for their wives, children, and the church. It is sometimes referred to as the "hierarchicalist" view because of

---

[1] Lera Boroditsky, "How Does Language Shape the Way We Think?" https://www.edge.org, 6.11.09

its emphasis on a hierarchy of relationships and at others "patriarchal" because of it emphasis on "father rule"—a term some complementarians would prefer to use. All of this should be done in love, seeking the best interests of the wife, family, and the church.

**Egalitarians** likewise believe in the equality of men and women before God, but differ in their understanding of what that looks like, believing that men and women are equal not only in person-hood before God but also in role capabilities. Therefore, both can fulfil roles of leadership within the home and the church as God gifts and enables. In practice, this means that marriage is a partnership between two equals and "roles" should be based on ability and gifting, not gender. Both are therefore personally responsible and accountable before God regarding life, marriage and the nurture of a family and may equally be involved in the life and ministry of the church. They would agree that just as all men are not gifted, called and enabled in the same way, neither are all women.

Having said that, there is, as I have suggested, a wide range of understanding within each group, much like we find in political parties, with extremes on both sides. There are extreme or hardline complementarians who place a strong emphasis on patriarchy, and there are extreme or hardline egalitarians who would border on feminism. On the other hand, some complementarians are almost egalitarian, and some egalitarians are fairly close to some complementarians. Each side would be happy at times to make use of language from the other side.

If you wish to read more, there is a limited bibliography at the back, along with a list of websites. My encouragement to you is, don't just accept what I have to say, but go, read, explore and reflect on both sides of the subject yourself. And, in doing so, don't just read your favourite or 'tribal' authors.

Above all, go to the scriptures and search them, wrestle with them to see whether these things are so. Find those who take a different approach, and take the time to discuss and reflect on the subject in-depth with them. You may or may not come to the same conclusion.[2] I trust and pray, that what I have written will be of help and encouragement to many.

---

[2] The conclusions I have come to here are my own and do not reflect the position of my church or the movement/stream of which it is a part.

# CHAPTER ONE
## *Exploring the Big Question*

One of the biggest questions in the church concerns the role of women. Some clearly state that the place and role of women is in the home, with no speaking or leadership roles within the church, or if they are allowed, only with women and children. Other's say that women can speak in some settings involving men and women but they cannot exercise leadership roles. The debate is also more pronounced and vociferous in the United States than it is in the United Kingdom. Nevertheless, it is by no means resolved. Some denominations and streams hold to the full involvement of women (some having done so well before the rise of feminism—more on that later), and others continue to restrict it.

Another important factor related to this debate is the growing number of able women who have been held back because areas of ministry were considered off-limits to them. No matter that their sense of calling was identical to that of any male. Not only that, many have been hurt by the attitudes and actions of some of those in leadership positions towards them and their gifts.

## *My Journey*

Before I go any further, it may be helpful to say something about my own journey—a journey which has taken me through various church backgrounds, traditions, theological thinking and experiences.

Having grown up in a Strict Baptist setting (not "church," we were "chapel" people), I came to saving faith in Christ in an Assemblies of God church in my mid-teens and spent the early part of my Christian life there. During my time there, I sensed the call of God into the ministry and was encouraged to get involved in many aspects of church life, ministry, and mission, from Sunday School work to evangelism, from leading worship to preaching.

My journey since then has taken me through involvement, ministry, and leadership in a United Reformed/Methodist Church, planting a church, and membership and ministry in a Salt and Light Ministries church. There I became an elder with responsibility for one of the area congregations. I was later involved in transitioning it into a church. Some years later, following a clear prophetic word, I was privileged to lead the church in joining with the local Newfrontiers church, where my wife and I continue to worship and serve.

Over the years, I have done theological and pastoral training with the Assemblies of God, masters level at the Wales Evangelical School of Theology (now Union), and Westminster Theological Centre (Cheltenham). I have participated in a stream theological forum and been involved in leading and teaching on a foundational theology course. I have also had the opportunity to experience and minister in different denominations and church cultures in Romania, Kenya, and the Democratic Republic of Congo, as well as ministry in a variety of local churches in the UK.

Quite a journey, and certainly not the journey I anticipated when I first heard the call of God and started in ministry all those years ago! If you know anything about the denominations and streams that I've been involved with, you will realise that I have traversed a variety of theological persuasions and traditions from Hyper-Calvinism to Arminianism; Cessationist to Pentecostal/Charismatic, as well as various forms of church government and practice: itinerant ministries; female pastor, male pastor; male and female eldership; male eldership; baptist, congregational, presbyterian, and apostolic/five-fold ministry! One of the things I can say is that I have seen and known the blessing of God in every situation, and I thank God for the people, churches, ministry, encouragement, and experiences in every one of them.

One of the questions that evangelicals and charismatics/Pentecostals sometimes struggle with is: how can God bless those who think differently? After all, don't we have the truth or experience? Don't we have the right church government, etc.? So, Baptists may struggle at times with Anglicans over baptism, Congregationalists with Presbyterians over church government, etc. At the time of the charismatic renewal in the 1980s, some Pentecostals struggled with the outbreak of the pentecostal/charismatic blessing in the historic denominations—denominations many had been forced out of due to their experience of the Spirit. How could God do that? Yet God has and he does. He is no respecter of persons, denominations, or structures. For me, with my rather narrow background, the journey has been an eye-opener. I believe God led me the way he did to show me something of how he works in and through those who love him and his word, are open to his Spirit and seek to honour the Lord Jesus Christ, have a passion for him and his purposes, and who exhibit "faith working through love" (Gal 5:6).

Throughout my journey, as you can well imagine, I have wrestled with the role of women in the life and ministry of the church. There have been times when I would have to admit to being pragmatic about it. At others, though, I have held quite strong complementarian views. In recent years, the subject has come up again, and I have found myself wrestling with it and wanting to be clear in my own mind. In many ways, being pragmatic didn't answer the question—it was avoiding it. Also, I needed to be clear for the sake of the church, both men and women. Especially the women.

In doing so, I know only too well the tension of picking up a book and reading one side of the argument and thinking, "yes, that's it," and then picking up another and reading the other side of the argument and thinking, "yes, yes, that's it," to that too! Each digging deeper, each seeming to have a point. Each seeming to be biblical. One moment a complementarian, the next an egalitarian!

The reality is that arguments read within the bubble of our own experience can end up being circular, and self-affirming, while reading the other side can be both challenging and discomforting as we realise the argument is not without some truth after all, or as flawed as we thought it to be. Sitting on the fence is not easy. Ultimately, we all need to land somewhere and, having done so, respect and honour those who think differently.

## *The Big Question*

Back to our question, what can women be and do in the church today? Or more to the point, can a woman be and do everything a man can? Can they preach and teach both women and men? Can they be pastors, elders, or overseers? Can a woman be the lead elder or senior pastor? Are there any restrictions placed on women about what they can do? They are big and important questions.

Depending on the denomination or stream you come from, it will no doubt influence your response to it. In some areas of the church, it has never been a problem; in others, it is a big issue. For still others, there has been some "to-ing" and "fro-ing" on the subject over the years as the leadership of the church or denomination has changed (i.e. the Southern Baptists in the United States). The Wesleyans, though, were ordaining women as far back as 1853. The Salvation Army saw Catherine Booth preaching from the beginning in 1865, as equality was always a founding belief. The Nazarenes, likewise, since their founding in 1908; the Free Methodists since 1911; and the Assemblies of God since 1914. What's more, we'll find out that the role of women goes back much further than we think, way before there was any talk of feminism or inclusivity. In Chapter Eight, Exploring Church History, we'll be taking a closer look at the role of women throughout church history—something I found both inspiring and challenging and hope you will too.

So, there's nothing new here. It cannot be put down to a cultural shift, political correctness, being 'woke' or the result of feminism. Much of what has been written in recent years on the complementarian role of men and women, both in church and the family, has more to do with the church wanting to shore up marriages and families against the seeming onslaught of a world intent on destroying them. The danger then is that we go in the other direction and develop a siege mentality, and the doctrine we develop has more to do with that, than with what scripture says, as texts are overworked and made to fulfil an agenda. In Chapter Six, Exploring the Problem Passages, we'll take a little bit of time to look at the origin and development of this argument.

Sadly, over time, it has become a controversial and contentious issue, with strong views being expressed on both sides. The rhetoric at times has been shocking. As such, it has the potential to cause division as lines are drawn and judgements are made. Unfortunately, it has not been helped by the suggestion that those who believe that women can fulfil some or even all roles, do not believe in the authority of scripture, and are "clearly in conflict with God's word." Neither does it help to suggest that they are more likely to compromise the gospel, or downplay it in some way to make it possible, or that they are Arminians (yes, I've read that kind of thing, as if being Reformed and holding to "biblical womanhood" means that you hold the theological high ground, and are the ones who are truly orthodox, and able to make the final judgement call). Worse is the accusation that any Christian who holds such a view is considered to be an outright liberal with a feminist agenda, and if we cave in on this, then the next thing will be sexuality.[3]

It doesn't end there. Worse still, is the accusation that "Pagan ideas underlie evangelical egalitarianism," and that it will lead to a "denial of the gospel" and the "disintegration of marriage in our culture."[4] In the recent discussion in May

---

3 See Wayne Grudem, *Evangelical Feminism, A New Path to Liberalism?* (Wheaton, IL: Crossway, 2016).

4 Duncan and Stinson, quoted in "A New Case for Female Elders: An Analytical Reformed-Evangelical Approach" (University of South Africa, 2013). 85.

2021 over a well-known church in the United States ordaining women pastors, someone on Twitter described it as, "open rebellion against Christ our King, and high treason against his sovereignty."[5] Enough said.

Such statements and accusations are not helpful. If you take the time and make the effort to look and listen, you'll find people on both sides of the debate who have a high view of scripture and regard the Word in the same way that you do. In his book, *Man and Woman, One in Christ*, Philip Payne says,

> "My belief in both inerrancy and the equality of man and woman may seem absurd to many on each side... How can a thinking textual critic with an enlightened egalitarian view still cling to the notion of biblical inerrancy? Conversely, how can someone who believes everything taught by God's inspired Word come to the position that the bible permits women to teach and exercise authority over men in the church?"[6]

The first premise in this discussion is that we truly honour and respect one another as brothers and sisters in Christ. That we do not throw stones at each other, or "diss" one another as the younger generation would say, or worse still, "cancel" them out and shout them down as nobodies. This is of primary importance, otherwise, we end up digging our trenches and throwing hand grenades at one another, and that is not helpful or edifying, and neither is it a good witness.

---

5 B. H. Carroll quote on Twitter @AdamGreenway in response to Saddleback ordaining female pastors, 9.05.2021.

6 Philip Payne, *Man and Woman, One in Christ, An Exegetical and Theological Study of Paul's Letters* (Grand Rapids, MI: Zondervan, 2015). Epub: Paragraph: My Odessey.

## *Gender Stereotyping*

Many of us will have grown up with some kind of gender stereotyping in which we have been conditioned to think of male and female roles in particular ways, i.e., men are good at this and are bad at that. Women, likewise (if you are old enough, think of adverts for household products). The argument goes along the lines that men like problem-solving, fixing things, being outdoors, love reasoning, are very competitive, are natural leaders, are not given to much emotion, etc. Women, on the other hand, are organisers. They like cooking and relationships; they are highly emotional and more spiritual; they enjoy decorating; they love children; they are home-makers and indoor types, and they like to be followers rather than leaders.[7] In other words, men lead and women follow; men provide and protect, while women feed and nurture. Men are rational, women are intuitive. Some would go as far as to say that such an approach subsumes the female within the male, or under the male, and therefore the woman is derived from and gets her sense of being and purpose from the man. Men are first, and women are second.

The big danger here is in reading our Bibles through gender-stereotyped, culturally-conditioned, 21st-century lenses and then assuming that we are interpreting scripture correctly. I was one of those. That is how I grew up. That is what I was taught. I was culturally conditioned. Several years ago, I remember being asked by a church leader if I was a "new man," a question that was loaded with cultural conditioning. The fact is, the modern Biblical Manhood and Womanhood movement is a culturally conditioned movement, both in its response to a changing world and in its teaching of the roles

---

[7] Kadi Cole, *Developing Female Leaders* (Nashville, TN: Thomas Nelson, 2019), Kindle Edition, loc 499, Conditioning.

of men and women. Rachel Green Millar (a mild complementarian—my description, not hers), notes in her book, *Beyond Authority and Submission,* that ideas that have more to do with the Greeks, Romans, and Victorians than they do with the scriptures have found their way into the Biblical Manhood and Womanhood movement.[8] For this reason, though she leans in that direction, she says she is not happy to call herself a complementarian. Interesting.

## *Baggage*

In coming to scripture and seeking to understand it, we need to recognise that most of us carry some form of baggage that affects the way we read, interpret and apply scripture. The challenge throughout my life and ministry has been to dare to get beyond my preconceived ideas, to get past my cultural conditioning, and to stand back and try to understand scripture as it was originally intended—to inquire what scripture meant on its first hearing, before attempting to comprehend what it might be saying to us today. That is not liberalism. It is also not what has been dubbed "progressive Christianity," which is simply old-fashioned liberalism disguised—a form of belief that stripped people of their faith, emptied churches, and led to the demise of historic denominations. It is rather, what scripture calls us to. We only have to stop and think of Jesus, who challenged those of his generation who were misreading and misapplying the scriptures with detrimental effect. It happens in every generation.

The questions each one of us must ask of ourselves are: are we rooted in the "God-breathed" word of Scripture?

---

[8] Rachel Green Millar, *Beyond Authority and Submission* (Phillipsburg, NJ: P & R Publishing, 2019). Kindle Edition: Introduction, Who Believes That?

Where does our theology come from? How much of it has to do with the prevailing ideas of the day and the part of the world and culture we find ourselves in?[9] Like some politicians today, we can also live in a bubble, disconnected from the world at large, deeming what we believe to be the truth, the whole truth, and nothing but the truth.

Another way of putting it might be, are we prepared to "listen to the Spirit" in the text,[10] rather than through our own cultural preconditioning. It's not always easy. It's also risky. It may cost you. Before we dig in, may I ask you, what is your background? Where did you grow up? How have you been taught? What is your preconditioning? How do you read the scriptures? Have you ever given it a thought? Are you aware of it? What stereotyping and baggage do you need the Spirit's help to lay aside to be able to hear what the Spirit might be saying?

## *Abuse*

Another reason we need to take a fresh and honest look at this subject is due to abuse in the church and the home.

**Abuse in the church.** In coming to it, I have become increasingly aware that there are women who have felt put down by men within the church. As if somehow, they are lesser people, having less intelligence and ability. On the other hand, if they have dared to say something, they have been treated as rebellious and accused of being "Jezebelic"—a

---

9  Michael F. Bird. "Some Parts of Evangelicalism Do Not Need to be Deconstructed… They Need to be Destroyed."
Https//michaelfbird.substack.com/p/some-parts-of-evangelicalism-do-not Accessed 25.11.2021

10  Gordon Fee, *Listening to the Spirit in the Text* (Grand Rapids, MI: Wm B Erdmans), 2000.

sure way to silence a woman who desires to have a good heart before God.

The idea of a Jezebelic spirit comes from the story of Jezebel in the Old Testament, who was a manipulative and controlling woman. This has been something thrown at strong and confident women. There is such a thing, and a man can operate out of the wrong spirit too, but to label every strong woman as Jezebelic is patently wrong. It can be a sign of a weak male leader. The fact is, it does more harm than good. I have known women who have been labelled in that way, when in fact they were faithful and sound, possessing vision and faith, and were by no means Jezebelic.

**Abuse in the home.** Not only that, but there can be abuse in the home under the guise of headship, where the husband is unspiritual, unloving, selfish, controlling, demanding, and abusive—in other words, sinful. No consideration is given to the wife and how she feels, or what her desires might be. And all the decisions are made by the man, and for the man, and serve his desires and purposes.

Some have graciously lived with such abuse based on a wrongly perceived biblical understanding of love, authority, and submission; that is, male authority, female submission, or what has become known as the doctrine of headship—more on that later. Nevertheless, they carry a woundedness that runs deep and needs to be listened to. Sadly, too many have suffered abuse at the hands of authoritarian men, and their experiences have been covered over under some spiritual guise.[11] If you have any doubts about this, I encourage you to read Kevin Giles's *The Headship of Men and the Abuse of Women*.

---

[11] Kevin Giles, *The Headship of Men and the Abuse of Women* (Eugene, Or: Cascade Books, Wipf and Stock), 2020.

Having said that, please note that I am not saying that complementarianism in and of itself will lead to abuse. That would be wrong. Many who hold to it and teach it, abhor and oppose any kind of control, exploitation, and oppression, and there are many good complementarian marriages. But, abuse exists, and wherever it has taken place, it needs to be recognised, repented of, and rectified. And where the structures aid and abet, they need to be changed. If you have been hurt or abused in any way, please do talk to somebody. Please do seek professional help and healing. If you are in a situation where that is the case right now, please get some help immediately.

## *Starting on the Wrong Foot*

The three main questions involved in the debate are: What roles can women fulfil in the church? Were there women leaders in the early church? Was every role open to them, or were there some limitations, and if there were, do they still apply today?

In seeking to understand the role of women in the church, many have turned to what have become known as the controversial passages of scripture—scriptures such as 1 Timothy 2:11-15, "I do not allow a woman to teach or to have authority over a man; instead, she is to remain quiet," or 1 Corinthians 14:33,34, "As in all the churches of the saints, the women should be silent in the churches, for they are not permitted to speak, but are to submit themselves, as the law also says"—the immediately presumed answers to the questions. Scripture says it, that's it; you can't get plainer than that. Many books and websites do just that—question posed, question answered. Problem solved, let's move on—if only.

The problem with this approach is that it fails to take into account the whole of scripture. It also leads to confirmation bias, as certain texts are cherry-picked to confirm our point of view. Books are written focusing almost entirely on 1 Timothy 2:11-15 as if no other scripture spoke to the subject. This is nothing other than a form of proof-texting.[12] The result is that we start off on the wrong foot, blinded by the seeming answer and prevented from seeing if anything else might be there—or as the old saying has it, we can't see the wood for the trees. Blinded by the seeming clarity, strength, and authority of a few verses, we draw our conclusions. And surely, two or three witnesses are enough. The Bible, though, consists of sixty-six books, all of which Paul says are "God-breathed" and profitable for instruction and training.

Rather than starting with the so-called difficult passages of scripture, I am proposing that it would be better to pose the question differently and ask, *what did women do in the Bible*? In doing so, we might well be surprised. My encouragement is to step back, change the lenses, and come afresh to the Scriptures—that we open our hearts and minds to all of Scripture and seek to hear what it has to say.

We begin the next chapter by exploring the roles that various women played in the Old Testament, followed by a chapter on women and the roles they played in the New Testament. Then we will take a trip back to the beginning to explore God's original intention, the impact of the Fall and how much the new creation changes things. From there, we will take a look at the nature of the New Testament Church, before moving on to a chapter exploring the problem passages. In Chapter Seven, we will explore the questions and issues regarding women and eldership. After that, we will look at

---

12 Kevin Giles, "Women in the Church: A Rejoinder to Andreas Kostenberger," (Evangelical Quarterly, 73:3, 2001), 239.

some of the women and the roles they fulfilled throughout church history, followed by some closing thoughts in the last chapter.

# CHAPTER TWO

## *Exploring the Role of Women in the Old Testament*

Let's start with a quick overview of some of the women and the roles they fulfilled in the Old Testament—a bird's eye view, as it were. In doing so, we need to remind ourselves that the world of the Bible was very different to the one we find ourselves in. Among the people of God, and in the cultures and nations beyond, society was largely patriarchal in structure. The man, to use modern language, wore the trousers, was the head of the home, was the leader of the nation and the arbiter of all things. For whatever reason, and that's another subject, that's the way things were. This makes things all the more interesting as we discover the various women in the story of Israel and the roles they fulfilled under the Old Covenant. Many of these could easily be expanded on. For the sake of time and space, I will make a few brief comments appropriate to the discussion.

**Eve.** Herbert Lockyer describes Eve as a "woman of distinction."[13] I like that. We so easily pass over her, yet she, like

---

13  https://www.biblegateway.com/resources/all-women-bible/Eve

Adam, holds an important part in the unfolding story of humanity. Unfortunately, scripture says very little about her apart from the fact that she, like Adam, was created in the image of God. That God created her as a "helper" for Adam and a partner for him in the stewarding of creation (we'll talk more about what that means later). As Adam was the first man, Eve was the first woman. Together, they were "humanity." She was perfect, complete, the first to give birth, the first mother. The name Eve means the "mother of all living" (Gen 3:16,20), a name given to her by Adam. It was a name full of prophetic significance, prophetic of the life that would flow from her, both naturally and redemptively. Though she, along with Adam, sinned and fell short of God's glory, one day, through the seed of a woman, sin would be defeated and creation restored.

**Sarah.** Sarah was the wife of Abraham. Her name meant "princess." Along with Abraham, they raised the family that was to become the nation of Israel. More still, Sarah would be "the mother of nations" (Gen 17:16 NIV). Despite her doubts, scripture tells us that Sarah was a woman of faith and, by faith, "received power to conceive offspring, even though she was past the age, since she considered that the one who had promised was faithful. Therefore, from one man—in fact, from one as good as dead—came offspring as numerous as the stars of the sky and as innumerable as the grains of sand along the seashore" (Hebrews 11:11-12). Isaiah was inspired to write, "Look to Abraham your father, and to Sarah who gave birth to you" (Isaiah 51:2). In his letter to the Galatians, Paul referred to Sarah as a symbol of the new covenant (Galatians 4:21-33).

**Miriam.** Miriam was a prophetess and leader of the people of God, *alongside* Moses and Aaron. It wouldn't be too much of a stretch to suggest that they were Israel's "eldership" at that time (Micah 6:4). Together, they were responsible for leading the people of God. Miriam is described as a prophetess, someone raised up by God to proclaim the will and purposes of God. She led Israel in worship and celebration, music and dancing, praise and proclamation (Ex 15:20, 21). It may be that such a ministry is lost on us today, but it was of vital importance in the life of Israel.

**The Five Daughters of Zelophehad.** Five women who most people have never heard of. Zelophehad, their father, had died, leaving five unmarried daughters, with no husbands or brothers, and therefore without any rights. In a section on inheritance in Numbers, these five daughters, against all odds, decided to take matters to the top. They stepped out of their homes where they should have stayed, the destiny imposed on them, and went up to the Tent of Meeting to seek out and speak personally to "Moses, the priest Eleazar, the leaders, and the entire community at the entrance to the tent of meeting" (Num 27:2), about their rights, or rather the lack of them. They outline their case, speaking with some determination (Num 27:3,4). They recognise the current law is inadequate, and recognising that God's law is just, or aims to be, they have no hesitation in arguing their point, that it is treating them unfairly, and go on to support it with compelling arguments. Moses took the matter to God. God agreed with them and the law was changed (Num 27:5-11). They are not condemned by God or Moses for what they did.

**Deborah.** Deborah was a married woman who God raised up to be a prophet and judge, or ruler, what we might call a primary leader, and men were accountable to her. She was a general and made military decisions (Judges 4:5-24; 5:15). Men and women came to her in the same way they did with Samuel for judgements (Judges 4:4,5). Prophecy was not so much about fore-telling, as forth-telling, a telling forth of

God's word. The book of Judges tells us that the villages were deserted in Israel until Deborah arose as a "mother in Israel," a title that was an indication of authority (Judges 5:7) and one that would be picked up hundreds of years later to describe women who were influential in the revivals of the nineteenth century. She also prophesied a major victory in the conquest of Canaan. While such a woman was rare, Scripture nowhere says that this should not have happened, or that it was for the lack of a man—as if she was God's second choice; and neither does it condemn her. It could be argued that the story is included in the Bible as a denial of the subordination of women and that it demonstrates that God does not see women as inferior or unable to lead.

Now some complementarians struggle with Deborah. They don't know what to do with her. She doesn't fit their particular mould. Their response is to say that Deborah was a woman of the Old Covenant and that the New Covenant has replaced it, so whatever Deborah did is irrelevant. That seems to be a strange way of reading the New Covenant. As we will see later, the New Covenant, rather than closing things down, releases and opens things up in regard to the role of women in the life and ministry of the church.

**Jael.** The story of Jael is brief and difficult for modern thinking and sensibilities. An obscure woman, Jael, is known as a woman who took initiative and killed Sisera, the general of a foreign army, who was fleeing for his life after they had been defeated (Judges 4:17-22; 5:24-27). Scripture concludes the events of that day by saying, "That day God subdued King Jabin of Canaan before the Israelites" (Judges 4:23). Deborah then speaks of her in her song, "Most blessed of women is Jael, the wife of Heber the Kenite; she is most blessed among tent-dwelling women" (Judges 5:24).

**Naomi.** Naomi seems to get a lot of bad press. I'm not sure that it's justified. She must have been an amazing woman considering all that she went through—famine, moving to a foreign land, the loss of her husband and then her two sons. Nevertheless, through her pain, she still maintains faith in God, though she feels God has dealt bitterly with her (Ruth 1:20,21). Her faith and testimony are such that Ruth is prepared to leave her family, her country, her gods, and all that she knows, and go with Naomi to serve the God of Israel. Staggering!

**Ruth.** Ruth was a Moabitess, a loyal and faithful woman who chose to leave everything she knew; her family, her home, her religion, and follow Israel's God. In doing so, unbeknown to her, she would one day become King David's great grandmother. Not only that, but she gets a mention in the genealogy of Jesus in Matthew 1 and a book named after her in the Hebrew scriptures! Now that's saying something!

**Esther.** Esther was a woman on whom God's hand rested. A woman born for a purpose. Esther became a queen and had incredible influence, and from her story, we get the well-known verse, "Who knows whether you have come to the kingdom for such a time as this?" (Esther 4:14 NKJV). There is, in every sense of the word, the idea that this was Esther's destiny, that she was born for this important and massively influential role. Esther was a woman of courage, faith, wisdom, and initiative. In modern-day language, we would say she was a stateswoman. Though there are no specific references to Divine revelation or prophetic words in the book of Esther, we do see God's hand at work through her and those around her, and the book becomes part of "the story of

God" breathed out by the Spirit.[14] A story that has been heard by and helped countless generations of his people.

**The unnamed woman of Abel Beth Maacah** was a woman who successfully negotiated with a military general for the deliverance of the town she lived in (2 Sam 20:14-24).

**Rahab.** Rahab was a prostitute who became a woman of faith in the God of Israel. She took in two spies sent out by Joshua to check out the land and hid them without seeking the permission or assistance of anyone in authority. She also sent those looking for them off in another direction. Rahab then freed the spies by lowering them by rope from her house on the city wall.

Rahab prophesied Israel's occupation of the land, saying, "I know that the Lord has given you this land and that the terror of you has fallen on us, and everyone who lives in the land is panicking because of you. For we have heard how the Lord dried up the water of the Red Sea before you when you came out of Egypt, and what you did to Sihon and Og, the two Amorite kings you completely destroyed across the Jordan. When we heard this, we lost heart, and everyone's courage failed because of you, for the Lord your God is God in heaven above and on earth below" (Joshua 2:9-11). She was saved and delivered from the judgement that came upon Jericho and is included in the genealogy of Jesus and the grand list of heroes of the faith in Hebrews 11 (Joshua 2:1, 3; 6:17-25; Matt 1:5; Heb 11:31; James 2:25). That's something!

**Athaliah** ruled as queen in Judah from 842 to 836 BC, though we must add, not a good one (2 Kings 11:3). That shouldn't be taken to say that God does not want women to

---

14 Gregory A Boyd, *Inspired Imperfection: How the Bible's Problems Enhance its Divine Authority*, (Minneapolis, MN: Fortress Press, 2020). Xxi.

be in leadership. That would be a bad argument, as there were plenty of bad men who were kings!

**Huldah.** Huldah was a prophet and royal adviser (2 Chron 34:14-33; 2 Kings 22:8-20; 23:1-25). When the scroll of the Law was found in the Temple, she was called upon to authenticate it and helped spark religious reform in the days of Josiah. What is amazing is that she was the only person who understood Torah and was able to teach it at that time (2 Kings 22:14–20; 2 Chronicles 34:22–28). Huldah prophesied the end of Israel's occupation of the land.

**Sheerah** built a town—no mean feat (1 Chron 7:24)!

**The daughters of Shallum** were involved in helping to rebuild the walls of Jerusalem (Neh 3:12).

**A great company of women.** The Psalmist speaks of a great company of women who proclaimed the good news: "The Lord announces the word, and the women who proclaim it are a mighty throng" (Psalm 68:11 NIV). "The Lord gives the word; the women who announce the news are a great host" (ESV), or as the NASB 2020 has it, "a great army." When God spoke his word, it was the women who took it up and proclaimed it, and what was it? The good news of what God has done for his people.

**An industrious woman.** The woman described in Proverbs 31:10-31 was far more than our traditional 'homemaker.' She was truly industrious, rising early, buying and selling, and working hard to provide for her family. She is full of wisdom and faithful instruction, and because of *her* reputation, her husband is respected at the city gate, where he sits among the elders.

Though women were deemed to be inferior to men in Jewish culture, they were not totally subjected to them, Judaism sought to lift them up and encourage their full and rightful involvement within their proper sphere. Although a man prayed, "Blessed art Thou O Lord our God, King of the Universe, who has not made me a woman," and the women responded, "Blessed art Thou O Lord our God, King of the universe, who hast made me according to Thy will," prayers instituted after Ezra's revival, women in Jewish culture were generally held in higher esteem and with greater dignity than those in the cultures around them. And though, largely speaking, their influence was seen to be in the home, they were not entirely ruled out of society.[15]

Admittedly, there are not as many women as men, but even in this brief overview of Old Testament examples, it would appear that women could adequately fulfil a whole range of roles. In fact, they could fulfil almost any role that men could fulfil, which begs the question, what couldn't they do? The only role that was closed to a woman in the Old Testament was that of the priest, but even that was not open to all men but limited to a particular group of men. Nevertheless, Israel was called as a people to be a "kingdom of priests" (Ex 19:5-8; Is 61:6), something that is much debated as to its meaning, yet however we understand it, it must by definition include women.

Therefore, we can conclude that before we reach the New Testament, Judaism was open to and had experienced women fulfilling a whole range of roles, from prophets to judges, counsellors, worship leaders, and rulers. Though there may not have been so many involved in such roles as men, that certainly should not be taken to mean that they could not or should not. To quote Matthew Schlimm, "Interspersed among the patriarchal voices are daring statements

---

15  Charles C. Ryrie, *The Role of Women in the Church* (Nashville, TN: B & H Publishing, 1958, 2011), Ebook: Chapter 1, Section: The Status of Women in Judaism.

that affirm the great dignity and worth of women."[16] Though their world and the world around them was patriarchal the Bible cannot be said to be "consistently patriarchal," and "it neither defends not theologizes that presupposition."[17]

**Another Day.** Before we leave the Old Testament, we need to stop and take note of Joel's prophecy about another day, a different generation, when the Spirit would be poured out on all flesh, and the sons and daughters would prophesy, "I will even pour out my Spirit on all humanity; then your sons and your daughters will prophesy... I will even pour out my Spirit on the male and female slaves in those days" (Joel 2:28,29). Craig Keener observes that prophesying in the Old Testament was "the most common form of ministry with respect to declaring God's word."[18] In fact, much of what is referred to today as prophecy, in Pentecostal/Charismatic circles, is more likely to fall into the categories of words of knowledge or wisdom than prophecy. In scripture, prophecy is connected to the Word, to the teaching of it. It is more of a forth-telling than a fore-telling, though it could and frequently did include both. The old puritans of the 1500s used to think of preaching as prophesying, though, of course, that itself is too limiting.[19] As Moses wished that all the Lord's people were prophets, Joel makes it abundantly clear that

---

[16] Matthew Richard Schlimm, *This Strange and Sacred Scripture: Wrestling with the Old Testament and Its Oddities* (Grand Rapids, MI: Baker Academic, 2015), 1,2, 99.

[17] GordonFee, *Listening to the Spirit in the Text* (Grand Rapids, MI: Wm B Erdmans Publishing Co. 2000), 81.

[18] Craig Keener, *Two Views on Women in Ministry* (Grand Rapids, MI: Zondervan, 2001,2005), 207.

[19] William Perkins, *The Art of Prophesying* (Digital Puritan Press, n.d.).

that is exactly God's intention and that there should be equality in our experience and ministry of the Spirit, both male and female.

So what of the New Testament?

# CHAPTER THREE
## *Exploring the Role of Women in the New Testament*

In turning to the New Testament, we find that women were actively involved in the life and ministry of Jesus and the birth and growth of the early church. We also discover that the roles they played were not minor, but crucial. They were there right from the beginning. Again, for the sake of time and space, this will be a 'fly by' as it were. I'll make some observations along the way, as I think that might be helpful here. More could be said, but it will give us an overview of the various women and their roles in the New Testament and some of the dynamics of how we read and understand the text.

**Elizabeth and Mary.** As the New Covenant story begins to unfold, we find Elizabeth and Mary having encounters with the Holy Spirit and speaking forth the word of God (Luke 1:39-45; 46-55). Though Luke does not say Mary is prophesying, he regarded the Spirit's fullness as showing up through prophetic utterance and therefore finds no need to clarify every utterance as prophetic.

**Anna.** Anna was a prophetess, who functioned like an Old Testament prophet[20] and spoke prophetically of Jesus when he was brought into the temple (Luke 2:36-38). Though she appears briefly in the pages of scripture, her role is nonetheless important.

**Women financed the ministry of Jesus.** Luke tells us that "women were helping to support them out of their own means" (Luke 8:1-3 NIV). All ministry needs resourcing, and they, the women, resourced the ministry of Jesus and his team.

**Women who were disciples of Jesus.** This was unusual for the culture of the day. Jewish women rarely, if ever, had the opportunity to study with teachers of the Law in the way that men did. Luke tells us that Jesus took his twelve disciples along with "some women… Mary… Joanna, the wife of Chuza… Susanna, and many others who were contributing to their support from their private means" (Luke 8:1-3 NASB 2020; see also Luke 10:39; Matthew 27:55–56; Mark 15:40–41). It was radical and counter-cultural, even scandalous. Unfortunately, the way it reads in many of our bibles, "many others" can sound like many men and women, when the reference is to "many women." Ben Witherington says, "Jesus is the first person in early Judaism to have female disciples, much less travelling female disciples."[21] Jesus treated women not only with care and respect, affirming their dignity and status, he also gave them permission to be and do all that he wanted them to.

---

20 Schreiner, T. Linda L. Belleville, Craig L. Blomberg, and Craig S. Keener, *Two Views on Women in Ministry* (Grand Rapids, MI: Zondervan, 2005), 276.

21 https://margmowczko.com/ben-witherington-on-jesus-and-women/

**Mary,** Luke tells us, sat at the feet of Jesus, which was a posture of learning, the posture of a disciple (Luke 10:38-42). Though Jesus chose twelve male disciples, any idea that this means he supported male headship is by inference only, and cannot be substantiated. He related to women in the same way he did to men. In his gospel, Luke demonstrates the full implications of the gospel regarding women by emphasising the role of women at both the beginning and the end of his gospel, and throughout his narrative as he couples together numerous stories involving men and women. Deliberate? I think so!

**Women were the first to meet Jesus risen from the dead.** They were the first witnesses to the resurrection and the first to proclaim it, something radical for that time as the testimony of a woman was not accepted in the courts (Matt 28:1-10; Mark 16:1-8; Luke 24:1-13; John 20:1-18).

**Mary and other women** were among the 120 there in the days leading up to Pentecost and experienced the coming of the Spirit in the same way as the disciples (Acts 1:12-14; 2:1-4). This is vitally important and something we can easily pass over. As Grenz and Kjesbo put it in their book, *Women in the Church*,

> "Women's participation in the Pentecost event has radical and far reaching implications. Not only did women receive Christ's commission as credible witnesses to the resurrection, but at Pentecost they also received the Spirit's power to carry out this central community responsibility. This means that women had received the same foundational qualifications for ministry as men in the New Testament church."[22]

---

22 Stanley J. Grenz and Denise Muir Kjesbo. *Women in the Church* (Downers Grove, IL: InterVarsity Press, 1995) Ch 3, Women in the Faith Community, Kindle location 868.

**Priscilla.** Priscilla was Paul's travelling companion and gave particular doctrinal instruction with her husband Aquila to Apollos at Ephesus (Acts 18:26). Correcting doctrine was not done by anyone but was considered to be the role of bishops or elders. We read of the church meeting in their home (1 Cor 16:19). When Paul wrote his second letter to Timothy in Ephesus, he sent greetings not only to Timothy but also to Priscilla and Aquila, as well as the household of Onesiphorus (2 Tim 1:2; 4:19). No other Christians in Ephesus are greeted. This begs the question, were these four people the leaders of the Ephesian church? In Paul's list of greetings to members of the church at Rome in the last chapter of Romans, Priscilla is listed first among 26 individuals (Rom 16:3-16). First! Again, does this indicate that Priscilla was also a leader in the church in Rome? Did they have a roving ministry? Whatever the answer, Priscilla was obviously influential and highly thought of by Paul.

**Junia** was highly esteemed among the apostles. It's generally agreed that it is not Junias (as it was at one time translated), which is a male name, but Junia, a female, that Paul is referring to (Romans 16:7). Though it is now widely accepted that it was a woman, the debate now centres on what the verse means; was Junia *an* apostle, or someone *highly regarded* by the apostles? We'll take a closer look at that later. Interestingly, in contrast to the modern debate, Junia's gender was not an issue in the patristic era. Origen assumed Paul's friend was a woman, and John Chrysostom held her in high regard even though he was not a supporter of women bishops.

**Euodia and Syntyche,** who are frequently thought of and remembered because of their disagreement, were highly esteemed by Paul and worked hard alongside the apostle as evangelists, something which involved both preaching and teaching (Phil 4:2-3).

**Phoebe** was a deacon and a church leader and was entrusted with taking Paul's letter to the church in Rome. The carrier of such a letter was more than a postman or woman, and there appears to be every reason to believe that she would have read it to the church and answered any questions about it. This would have required trust and confidence that Phoebe understood Paul's teaching. That she was well able to articulate and communicate it, and well able to answer any questions that might arise in doing so (Rom 16:1-2).[23] Philip Payne says,

> "The only person unambiguously identified by name and given a title for local church leader in the NT is Phoebe, and she may be given two such titles, 'deacon of the church of Cenchrea' and or 'leader (προστάτις) of many.' Consequently, the argument is spurious that since women are not given the title 'elder,' 'overseer,' or 'pastor' in the NT, they may not occupy those offices. The same logic if applied to Christian men would exclude all of them from the offices of overseer and pastor as well."[24]

Paul speaks of Phoebe as a *"diakonos"* (Rom 16:1), a Christian minister, a term he used of himself (Eph 3:7), and others involved in ministry (Eph 6:21; Col 1:7; 1 Tim 4:6). It's interesting how some translations gloss this by translating *"diakonos"*

---

23 Scot Mcknight, Reading *Romans Backwards: A Gospel in Search of Peace in the Midst of the Empire* (London: SCM Press, 2019).
24 Philip B Payne, "Is It True That In The NT No Women, Only Men, Are Identified By Name As Elders, Overseers, Or Pastors, And That Consequently Women Must Not Be Elders, Overseers, Or Pastors?" Online at: https://www.pbpayne.com/is-it-true-that-in-the-nt-no-women-only-men-are-identified-by-name-as-elders-overseers-or-pastors-and-that-consequently-women-must-not-be-elders-overseers-or-pastors/

as "minister" when it comes to men and "servant" in the case of women. Surely a case of gender bias. We should note that in many ways, Paul's affirmation of Phoebe is similar to that of his affirmation of Timothy to the church at Corinth (1 Cor 16:10,11). He knew her and the nature of her gospel ministry and was affirming of it. Paul describes the nature of her ministry to the church at Cenchreae as "a minister of the church," which suggests she was known and recognised as fulfilling, in modern terms, an "office" in the church. In Rom 16:2, Paul uses the word *"prostatis,"* translated as "helper" in many versions, to describe her, which is the feminine of a word for a leader, ruler, president or guardian, and in Greek and Roman society, a patron.

Phoebe may also have been an apostle. In his greeting to the church in Rome, Paul identifies himself and no others, as he does in some of his other letters, yet in Romans 1:5 he uses the plural, "through him we have received grace and apostleship…" There are no obvious referents in the introduction. Could it be that Phoebe was included as she not only delivered but read out the letter from Paul?[25]

**Mary, Lydia, Chloe, and Nympha,** among others, are listed as the heads of churches that met in their homes (Acts 12:12; 16:13-15, 40; Rom 16:1-5; 1 Cor 1:11; 16:19; Col 4:15). Some have argued that Paul was simply naming some of these as hosts or patrons of the church that met in their home, which is possible, but it would be unlike Paul to mention them without mentioning the person who led the church. Linda Belleville notes, "The homeowner in Greco-Roman times was in charge of any group that met in his or her domicile and was legally responsible for the group's activities."[26]

---

25 J David Millar, "What Can We Say About Phoebe". (Priscilla Papers, vol 25, No 2, 2011) 18.

26 Linda L. Belleville, "Women in Ministry: An Egalitarian

Gordon Fee, in *Listening to the Spirit in the Text*, says, "It would never have occurred to them that a person from outside the household would come in and lead... To put it plainly, the church is not likely to gather in a person's house unless the householder also functioned as its natural leader."[27]

**Tryphena, Tryphosa, and Persis** are commended by Paul as the Lord's workers in Romans 16:12. Paul mentions some ten women in this chapter alone!

**The mother of Rufus.** Paul values her as one who has been a mother to him (Rom 16:13).

**The daughters of Philip** were prophetesses (Acts 21:9). New Testament prophecy was more than giving someone a "word," it involved a communication of the heart of God that would bring encouragement, edification, or exhortation, and a woman's role in prophesying was identical and of equal value to that of a man.

**Many of the widows** were mighty women of prayer, what we might describe as prayer warriors (1 Tim 5:5).

**Women deacons**—if we agree that this can be translated as women deacons (1 Tim 3:11).

**Lois and Eunice.** Timothy's grandmother and mother were recognised by Paul as people of sincere and influential faith (2 Tim 1:15).

**The Elect Lady** (2 John). Though much debated, there seems to be no logic to the suggestion that this is a reference to the church. If it was, it would make the reference to her children redundant. It makes more sense to accept the address, or description, as it stands, "The elect lady."[28]

---

Perspective" in James R. Beck, ed., *Two Views on Women in Ministry* Rev. Ed. (Grand Rapids, MI: Zondervan, 2005), 56.

27 Fee, *Listening to the Spirit in the Text*, 73.

28 Stanley J. Grenz and Denise Muir Kjesbo, *Women in the Church*.

**Praying and prophesying.** In 1 Corinthians 11:5, we see women praying and prophesying in the meeting—this verse is frequently overlooked, or stands in the shadow of its more well-known negative counterpart in 1 Corinthians 14:34, about women being silent in church.

Along with the above, we then have Paul's encouragement for all to participate in the worship of the church via teaching, counselling, revelation, speaking in tongues, interpretation of tongues, etc. And all of this without any sense of prohibition, or distinguishing between a man's role and a woman's. This would suggest the full participation of women within such gatherings, with no area of ministry being off-limits to them (Rom 15:14; 1 Cor 14:26; Col 3:16).

Among Complementarians, there is an endeavour to make a distinction in the type of teaching that Paul is referring to here, setting it in contrast to what Paul is referring to in 1 Timothy 2:12: "I do not allow a woman to teach…" In Corinthians, it's considered to be level 101, as it were, whereas, in 1 Timothy 2, it's a higher grade, authoritative, doctrinal teaching. This doesn't bear weight. Paul makes no such distinction. All teaching must be rooted in the Word and be theological and doctrinal, whether to children, youth, or adults, male or female. Yes, there will be differing levels of ability in that, but Scripture will not allow us to make a distinction based on sex.

## *Summary*

In our brief survey, it becomes clear that the early church benefited greatly from the gifts and talents, perspectives and experiences of women working alongside men. In both the

---

Kindle loc: 1023.

Old and New Testaments, we find many examples of women exercising gifts, even leadership gifts and authority (including over men) as judges, prophets, teachers, apostles, and deacons. All of which is in contrast to what has become known as "biblical womanhood" in the last fifty or so years, which "confines women's primary role to house and family and forbids women all leadership roles over men in the church" and "owes as much (if not more) to Western cultural norms of the last 200 years than it does to the Bible."[29]

Having done a quick overview of the Old and New Testaments, let's now go back to the beginning, and see what God intended in the first place.

---

[29] Beth Allison Barr, "The Myth of Biblical Womanhood, A Perspective from Medieval Africa." 24th October 2018.

# CHAPTER FOUR
## *Exploring God's Original Intention*

Having done a quick survey, it would be good for us to back up and explore how God set things up at the beginning, especially as this is a go-to point for the complementarian. Several questions come to mind: What was God's intention for men and women when he created them? Were they created equal? Was there a hierarchy in their relationship with one another? In what way was Eve created as a helper? What happened, if anything, to their relationship at the Fall? And from there, to ask the question, what impact, if any, does the new creation now have upon it?

In Genesis 1-3 we read the story of the Creation and the Fall, a story that should be taken at face value. The writer tells us how God creates the heavens and the earth and then fashions them for a purpose and how he creates Adam and Eve, real people in his own image. Adam was made first from the dust of the earth, then a woman from Adam's rib. Adam names the woman Eve, and together they are the pinnacle of God's creation, enjoying a relationship with their Creator that no other part of it did. They were appointed as co-regents of creation, accountable to God. After some time (how long we are not told), Eve is tempted by the serpent, and she and Adam eat from the Tree of Knowledge of Good and Evil, and sin enters creation. This brought about the curse and changed the way they related to God, to one another, and to the earth.

**Made in the Image of God.** The first thing we note in Genesis 1:26 is that God made them both, male and female, in his image, not one more than the other. Both were made equally in the image of God. To suggest otherwise is a dangerous route to go down as it implies inferiority, potentially even a lower grade of human. The sad fact of the matter is that this has been the attitude at different times, in varying places and cultures, and sadly still exists in some areas today. Scripture states emphatically that male and female, are equally imaged after the image of God.

The question then arises, how do we see God? For some of us, it may be that we need to stop and think about our view of God. After all, Scripture frequently uses male language in relation to God—he, father, king, or husband. The conscious or unconscious outcome of that may be the exaltation of the male and the diminution of the female.

Though Scripture frequently uses male language when referring to God, we should not for one moment take that to mean that God is male. The consequence of such thinking is that being female is derived and therefore somehow less an image of God. Because God is Spirit, he is neither male nor female. Yes, he has chosen to reveal himself in human terms and through human culture. And yes, he took on human flesh in male form. But God is not human. Though there are many references throughout Scripture to God as a father, Scripture also uses mother terms to speak of God, i.e., how he would nurse them, gather them, and protect them (Deut 32:18; Is 49:15; 66:13; Ps 131:2; Matt 23:37). It is also important to remember that God is Father, Son, and Holy Spirit, with Spirit being a feminine word in Greek.

**Bone of his bone.** Secondly, the fact that Adam named Eve should not be taken to mean that he had authority and power over her, as some have suggested. She was flesh of his flesh and bone of his bones, taken from his side to be his co-worker in stewarding creation, not a lesser, or weaker, companion over whom he was to have the last say. In creating them male and female, there is no suggestion that the male was to be the head of the woman. That is something that is just not there and has to be read into the text. In fact, the text implies that Adam was in need because there was nothing comparable to him among the animal creation, and so Eve was created.

**A helper.** Thirdly, the translation "helper" or "helper suitable" in most versions does not reflect the full intention and strength of the original Hebrew (Gen 2:18). In our language, a "helper" is more akin to someone asking: "can you help me?" or "would you like me to help you with that?" In other words, you are the one who knows what you are doing and has the strength, but you require a little bit of assistance here and there—a "helping hand" as it were.

Some complementarians are happy to think of it in this way. But is this correct? The word used here is a translation of the Hebrew, *ezer kenegdo.* The phrase appears more than 20 times in the Old Testament and is usually found in reference to God, and we certainly wouldn't make such references to God in his relationship to humanity. According to David Freedman it would be better to translate it to say that woman is of *"a strength equal to"* Adam.[30] If so, it is hardly a phrase one would use to describe someone who was designed to be subordinate, or simply a "helper."

This means that we cannot interpret it as if Adam was the stronger and more equipped of the two but had some weak points that Eve would make up for. She was not someone who was there to fill the gaps in his humanity. No, she would be a helper who fully corresponded to him, someone who was truly his equal. Eve then, was far more than Adam's able 'assistant' or servant. As David Freedman concluded, "When God creates Eve from Adam's rib, His intent is that she will be—unlike the animals—'a power (or strength) equal to him.'"[31] Or in the words of Rabbi Schlomo Riskin, "We cannot partner with a lesser being whom we subdue."[32]

**Dominion.** Fourthly, both the man and the woman are equally charged with responsibility and accountability to God for stewarding creation (Gen 1:26-28). Adam was no more responsible to God than Eve, and Eve was not responsible to Adam in a secondary way. Both were held equally accountable and answerable to God. Original creation sets them up as equally made in the image of God and equally called to steward creation. *They* were to have dominion, not just the man. They were an equal partnership in serving God on the earth.

The modern idea of roles is not to be found here. There is no sense of male authority and female submission, that has to

---

[30] David Freedman, quoted in, *Women in the Church* by Grenz and Kjesbo. Kindle Loc: 1962.

[31] Quoted in, *Women in the Church*, by Grenz & Kjesbo. Kindle Loc: 1962.

[32] Quoted by Skip Moen, The Great Risk, https://skipmoen.com/2009/05/the-great-risk/

be read into the text. Any such order is a modern construction. Indeed, if it were to be found there, it would mean that such roles apply to the whole sphere of life, the home, the church, and society (i.e. children's work, police departments, education, government, etc.). The result of such thinking would be the exclusion of women from exercising authority in any setting (which is where some complementarians end up). In the creation story, men and women are not differentiated regarding their roles but their God-given natures, which leads us to the next point.

**Equal, but different.** Fifthly, at the same time, they are different. They are distinguished as male and female and are biologically and physically different. Not only that, there are differences in the way males and females think and feel, which means they both bring something different to the table. When the table has only one side, male or female around it, there is an imbalance.

According to the American Psychological Association, when it comes to business, women tend to have a more cooperative, participatory style of leading, whereas men tend to have a more "command and control" style. Men tend to be more task-oriented and directive, while women tend to be more democratic. Men are good at providing direction, while women encourage people to find their own direction.[33] The fact is we were made to complement one another, not compete with or do without the other sex.

Kevin Giles in his paper, *The Genesis of Equality*, sums it up well when he says,

"Thus what we have in this primary and definitive scriptural comment on the sexes is the strongest

---

[33] https://careeradvancementblog.com/male-female-leadership/

imaginable affirmation of the equal status of man and woman ("in the image of God he created them"), of male-female differentiation ("male and female he created them") and of their conjoint authority over creation ("let them have dominion"). Their equality cannot be taken simply to be a spiritual equality, an "equality before God."[34]

## *The Fall — A Distortion*

At some point after creation, the enemy appears in the garden, bringing temptation and the offer of 'godness.' Both Adam and Eve fell for it, and the consequences for them and creation were huge. The sad fact is that truth and reality became distorted through the Fall. Humanity's sin distorted God's design and intention in every sphere of life, resulting in the appearance of things that were not previously present, such as fear, mistrust, the desire for power over another, suppression and oppression as dominating and controlling structures entered the human experience. Relationships were turned on their head, and abuse followed. Since that day, what it means to be human has been distorted, and correspondingly, what it means to be male and female has been distorted.

The writer of Genesis quotes God describing the Fall's consequences on the woman's relationship to her husband as, "Your desire will be for your husband, yet he will rule over you" (Gen 3:16b). Complementarians interpret this to mean "bad rule" or "unloving rule," but this is not what the text says. The word for rule here is the normal word used for rule, whether by God or man and is not qualified by any statement

---

34 Kevin Giles, "The Genesis of Equality, Part 1," (Priscilla Papers, Vol 28, No 4, 2014). 1.

to make it say otherwise. And if man's rule over woman was a result of the Fall, then conversely he could not have ruled over her before the Fall.[35]

## *A New Creation Changes Everything, or Does It?*

When we turn to the pages of the New Testament, we discover a dramatic intervention as Christ steps into this world not only to bring salvation but recalibration, where, in Christ, life and relationships are reframed and restored in him. In Christ, the old way has been found wanting and judged. In him, the demarcations and distinctions of the realm of the Flesh have been overturned, and now, as Paul says, "There is no Jew or Greek, slave or free, male and female; since you are all one in Christ Jesus" (Gal 3:28). Everything has been renewed and reframed in Christ. But there is a problem here. Frequently, this verse is referenced and celebrated in relation to the obliterating of the old lines of the flesh that marked out Jew and Gentile, yet it goes on to use the same argument about male and female. It's not that Jew and Gentile or male and female don't exist; they obviously do, so what does it mean?

The New Testament is radical in its approach to relationships. In those days, husbands owned their wives and frequently treated them harshly, and we need to keep this in mind when reading Paul's letters. So, when Paul writes, "husbands love your wives as Christ loved the church, and wives submit to your husbands" in Eph 5:21-29, we need to remember that the wife already submitted to her husband. She had no choice in the matter, he ruled over her.

---

[35] Philip B. Payne, "The Bible Teaches the Equal Standing of Man and Woman." (Priscilla Papers, Vol 29, No 1, Winter 2015), 3.

Therefore, Paul was not asking something new of her but rather that it be done in a new way, that it be "done in the Lord." It's the command to the husband, though, that is truly radical, as he is being asked to love his wife as Christ loved the church—that's a radically high calling, and a radical word in the time it was given! In loving her in such a way, he would be honouring her, dignifying her, lifting her to an equal status with himself—a truly dynamic and powerful witness to the world.

The gospel, the good news of Jesus, changes everything. In Christ, we don't simply have redemption, but a new creation, a new creation that is both personal and relational. The old walls set up in the realm of the Flesh that divided us have been brought down, not only concerning the distinctions between Jew and Gentile, slave and free but also between male and female. That is not to say there is no such thing as male and female; there are; rather, in Christ we have creation restored and renewed, and no one is more privileged than another in our relationship to God and to one another.

Grenz and Kjesbo in their book, *Women in the Church*, quote F. F. Bruce, as saying,

> "No more restriction is implied in Paul's equalizing of the male and female in Christ than in his equalizing of the status of Jew and Gentile, or of slave and free person. If in ordinary life existence in Christ is manifested openly in the church fellowship, then if a Gentile may exercise spiritual leadership in the church as freely as a Jew, or a slave as freely as a citizen, why not a woman as freely as a man."[36]

---

[36] Grenz and Kjesbo, *Women in the Church.* Kindle location: 1173

Before we get to the so-called problem passages, we need to stop and take a look at the New Testament church, and ask: what was it like? How did it function? Does it have any bearing on the argument?

# CHAPTER FIVE

*Exploring the Nature of the New Testament Church*

As we progress, it would be helpful in exploring the role of women in the church to pause and take a brief look at the nature of the New Testament Church and at what happened in a New Testament Church meeting. Why? Because all of us are, in some way or other, culturally conditioned by our present experiences and it is easy to assume they were or are the norm. The danger with this is that we read back into the text things that were simply not there. The church of today is vastly different to the church we find in the New Testament. That's why there's always a struggle when we talk about restoring the church to a New Testament church. What exactly was it, and how far do you go?

**Buildings.** We make much of them, large and small, ornate and plain. They are useful, but the early church had no buildings they called churches, chapels, worship centres, or cathedrals. For the most part, they met in people's homes, in extended family settings, including singles and servants. These were usually limited by the number of people who would fit into the atrium—on average, thought to be about fifty. These groups may have come together at times in larger venues for what we would call a celebration or, to use an older term, a convocation. On this basis, we can say that it makes no sense to say that a woman can teach or lead in a home setting but not in "the church." Such a statement is a non-starter as the church was not a sanctified building with stained-glass windows and religious furniture.

**Worship.** When they met together for worship, they weren't structured in the way that our "services" or meetings are today, whether Anglican, Baptist, Methodist, Pentecostal, or Charismatic etc. There were no doubt things that were carried over from the synagogue, such as the reading of scripture and prayer, but they were not "services" as we would call them, with a few people at the front and everybody else passively partaking or observing. There was no prayer book or liturgy, written or unwritten. Most of them were in homes, and everyone was encouraged to participate. This is the context of Paul's encouragement to the church at Corinth: "When you come together, each one has a hymn, a teaching, a revelation, a tongue, or an interpretation" (1 Cor 14:26). There was an emphasis on the priesthood of all believers, therefore upon "whole-body" ministry. Each could freely approach God, and each could freely bring something from God for the benefit of the body. The worship was Spirit directed and Spirit energised (1 Cor 12-14).

Following a trip to Scotland, I was stirred by the story of the great Scottish Reformer, John Knox, a man I knew of, but had read little about. I decided to change that and bought some books to fill out my knowledge of him. He was a truly amazing man, called and gifted by God for such a time—if you've not read about him, I would encourage you to do so. What fascinated me was that during the spiritual reformation that took place in Scotland through what has been described as the "hidden advance of the gospel," there were no "church officers." There were ordinary everyday people from all walks of life, bakers, merchants, butchers, etc., who would speak from their hearts, exhort one another, and read the scriptures. That life and ministry existed within the body. This proved so valuable that when "regular churches" were eventually formed, the practice was continued, and it was written into the Book of Discipline that once a week such meetings were to be held that were similar to what is described in 1 Corinthians 14.[37] Perhaps that's something we need to reflect on.

**Priests.** There were no official priests. An objection that is sometimes raised concerning women in the ministry is that only men could be priests in the Old Testament. True. But, even the Old Testament spoke of Israel as a people, male and female, as a "kingdom of priests" (Ex 19:6). Time has moved on, and so has God's unfolding purpose in human history. Fulfilment has taken place. A greater revelation has been given. This is the New Testament era. The old has gone, the new has come. Jesus, our great high priest, has offered himself as the supreme sacrifice once and for all for sin. No more sacrifices for sin need to be made. The emphasis in the New Testament is on the priesthood of all believers, both men and women. Each has the right to minister before God, and to God, and to come from God with something for the people, regardless of their lineage, sex, or ethnicity. Peter says we are

---

[37] D. M. Lloyd-Jones, Ian H. Murray, *John Knox and the Reformation* (Edinburgh, UK: Banner of Truth, 2018), 116-118.

a royal, or holy priesthood, offering up spiritual sacrifices (1 Peter 2:5).

Then came what has been called, the great reversal. Sometime after Christianity was lawfully accepted (think Constantine), they stopped meeting in homes and met in buildings they called churches and cathedrals that became more and more ornate. These had altars set apart from the main body of the building, and the breaking of bread or communion now became a sacrifice that once again needed priests wearing special clothes to mediate between the people and God. This was a backward step, a return to an Old Testament way of thinking, and with it came a return to an all-male ministry.

**Denominations.** Today, there are estimated to be some 45,000 of them! Tragic really. There were no denominations in the early church, and therefore none of the structures that we may be familiar with today. There were no groups who thought that church government should be congregational, presbyterian, episcopal, or apostolic. There was no such thing as the clergy and laity (horrible terms!). They were all priests unto the Lord and had the right to minister. All those things are a product of time plus the challenges of church growth and the need to oversee, care for, and protect the church.

Some denominations arose to uphold the truth, or a specific truth (i.e., predestination or free will), worship in a particular manner (liturgical, open/free, charismatic), or over the meaning and mode of baptism (infant, adult; sprinkling or full immersion), or the nature of communion (i.e., real presence, sacraments or symbols), and so on.

Churches are also made up of imperfect people like you and me, people who have blind spots and are still growing in Christ. Sadly, some of those divisions and denominations will have come about because of pride, selfishness, stubbornness, and an inability to face up to and deal with relational conflict and process disagreement.

**Cultural and Social Distinctions.** There were no distinctions. None. The New Testament Church consisted of those who had responded to the gospel and had come to know Jesus Christ as Lord and Saviour. Jesus had said he would build his church. The concept was familiar. They were gatherings of people who came together for a particular purpose. Jesus likewise gathers his people together for a purpose. The church was the gathered community, people gathered from different walks of life, different national backgrounds, different cultures, and different strata of society, but "one (people) in Christ Jesus," a place where there was "no Jew or Greek, slave or free, male and female; since you are all one in Christ Jesus" (Gal 3:26-29). A place where the old distinctions and distortions that came in after the Fall and are part of the domain of the Flesh which has been judged in Christ and is passing away, no longer apply. They were a new creation in Christ, crafted once more in the image of God. As such, any idea of status or privilege based on an individual's ethnicity, wealth, or gender in the church was anathema, as it was contrary to the gospel.[38] At a time when women were considered the property of their fathers or husbands, with no civil rights or identity, Paul makes it clear that they were all equally God's children through faith in Christ Jesus.[39]

---

38 Payne, "The Bible Teaches the Equal Standing of Man and Woman," 5.

39 Jim Denison, "What should the Role of Women be in the Church" Online at:
denisonforum.org/resource/faith-questions/what-should-be-the-role-of-women-in-church

**Ministry.** Ministry in the New Testament church was not only something the body participated in but also served by a team of men and women who were gifted in various ways to aid the growth, discipleship, development, and expansion of the body, something many would call today apostolic ministry. So Paul says in Ephesians 4:11,12, "And he himself gave some to be apostles, some prophets, some evangelists, some pastors and teachers, equipping the saints for the work of the ministry, to build up the body of Christ." This four or five-fold ministry (depending on whether you see pastor/teacher as one or two gifts) was given and appointed by Christ to various individuals—it wasn't vested in one. Some see this as an itinerant ministry serving a group or groups of churches, others as within the local church. Either way, it refers to a church receiving a variety of ministries and gifting. Just as many today recognize that the concept of a one-man ministry is wrong, likewise, a one-woman ministry would be wrong. At times, it may be necessary, but it should not be the norm. We might also note here that the Bible has no categories as we know them of senior pastor or elder—that is not to say we should not have them—which leads me to my next observation.

**Church government/offices.** At some point in time, following the preaching of the gospel and the gathering of new converts, elders and deacons were recognised and appointed within the churches. Paul commissioned elders and sent Timothy and Titus to put elders in place. The focus in scripture is always on plurality, never on an individual ministry. It's also questionable whether we should interpret eldership as an office in the modern sense, as it is in some denominations today. It was all about serving, not positions of authority and lording it over others.

Nowhere in the New Testament do any of the authors outline a specific order of church government. The idea that there were titles or structures to be applied to all churches in all places at all times is just not there. We only need to consider that within the church at large, there are at least four or five different forms of church government, i.e., congregational, presbyterian, episcopal or apostolic, or a mix, and all argued from scripture. Yet the fact is, for all the biblical arguments that can be mustered for any one of them, the New Testament is not that clear. As theologian Scott McKnight says, "Many think their church order—presbyterian, episcopal, congregational—is the biblical view of church order. I wish we could enjoy confidence in what we are doing without 'blaming' it on the NT because the NT, frankly, is not that clear."[40]

Maybe it has to do with our modern mindset and its linear thinking, along with our givenness to creating structures, whereas in the New Testament the emphasis was on gifting and serving, and how best to facilitate that. Titles and power belonged to the old fallen order of this world that has been judged in Christ and is passing away. Those who belong to the new order were not to live that way. In the kingdom of God, all are equal in Christ, and all are gifted in some way to serve the whole. At the same time, all don't have the same gifts, some have greater gifts and differing measures of them than others, but there is an equality of responsibility. It would appear then, that any such structure would be light, not pronounced, all that was necessary for the proper functioning and health of the whole. Not only that, rather than being

---

[40] Scott McKnight, "Elders, Deacons or Bishops."
Https:/scotmcknight.substack.com/elders-deacons-or-bishops

fixed, there was an adaptability to it that allowed the body to flourish and grow as the Spirit directed.

**Church or family.** I wonder what your preferred description of church is? Paul's preferred description or dominant metaphor is that of a family, of siblings, brothers and sisters in Christ, sharing and doing life together. Not a church, but siblings in a place of mutuality. It was not a meeting they would go to, or an institution, or a club they would belong to, nor simply a gathering of friends; it was first and foremost a family being a family, learning how to do this new life together. This has a huge impact on how we think about church and the place and role of women in the church.

Speaking in this way, Paul makes use of the word *adelphoi,* a word that has been the source of much discussion in recent years. Traditionally, *adelphoi* has been translated as "brothers" in our older versions, or "brethren," a word which actually means "brothers and sisters" in even older versions. To the chagrin of traditionalists, many of our newer translations translate it as "brothers and sisters." Any translation that has gone down this route finds itself accused of giving in to the culture, of buying into a feminist agenda, political correctness, or "gender inclusivity." Yet, this is neither true nor fair.

There is a Greek word for brother, *adelphos*, and for sister, *adelphe,* but the Greek word, *"adelphoi,"* can mean "brothers" or "brothers and sisters." If translators are doing their job correctly, it's right for them to translate either as "brothers" or "brothers and sisters" as the context demands (sometimes it is acknowledged through a footnote as in the ESV). There are times when it is "brothers," but there are times when "brothers" is too narrow as the context relates to the whole people of God, both male and female. To translate it otherwise would not be accurate. If the women, the sisters, are simply subsumed under the title "brothers," they lose their identity. This reinforces the idea that men are first, and women are derived from men and get their identity and significance through men.

Recognising that the church is a family of brothers and sisters in Christ is vital, and therefore, it follows that having the correct language is of utmost importance. The church is not a "worship centre," or "preaching centre," etc., but primarily a family of brothers and sisters who are learning how to do life together as God's children in the Spirit. This means the sisters must be fully recognised and involved.

In his work, *When the Church was a Family*, Joseph Hellerman says,

> "… the preeminent social model that defined the Christian church was the strong-group Mediterranean family. God was the Father of the community. Christians were brothers and sisters. The group came first over the aspirations and desires of the individual. Family values—ranging from intense emotional attachment to the sharing of material goods to uncompromising family loyalty—determined the relational ethos of Christian behaviour."[41]

In that family, particularly in the Mediterranean, women would have had a prominent role.

---

[41] Joseph Hellerman, *When the Church Was a Family: Recapturing Jesus' Vision for Authentic Christian Community* (Nashville, TN: B & H Academic, 2009), 119.

## *People of the Spirit*

Gone then are the old markers that separated one group from another; gone are the old power structures that allowed some to rule over others. They were all priests. There was no longer the need for any kind of intermediary. They each had the right to come to God and minister to him. They each had the right to come from God and minister to others. They were a royal priesthood. This didn't mean they didn't need one another, that it was just them and God, "me and Jesus," rather, they were a people, a family, each gifted and enabled to seek and bring the heart of God to one another.

They were also people of the Spirit, previously the domain and experience of a few: kings, queens, prophets, judges, craftsmen, etc. Yet a day had been promised when the Spirit would be poured out on all kinds of flesh, both Jewish and Gentile flesh, old and young, male and female without any exception. The Spirit's coming would transcend the old era and truly enable all to participate together in the experience of the Spirit for the furtherance of the gospel and the encouragement and upbuilding of all. Many years before, Moses had said, on hearing that some individuals were prophesying in the camp, "Would that all the LORD's people were prophets, that the LORD would put his Spirit upon them" (Num 11:29 ESV)! Moses understood something about prophecy. That day had arrived at Pentecost.

Prophecy appears to have played a much bigger role in the New Testament churches than in modern-day ones, even Pentecostal and Charismatic ones. When they came together, Paul said, "you may all prophesy," both the men and the women. This prophesying again was more than what is seen in most churches today. It was a speaking forth of the word of God, of revelation regarding the word. It compares in some ways with an older generation in church history who used to think of preaching in this way and wrote books about the art of prophesying, though it should by no means be entirely identified with preaching.[42] In some way, prophecy was about speaking forth the word of God. They were more than a couple of sentences and more than a revelation about someone. Paul says prophecy edifies, encourages, and builds up.

When Paul said, "What then, brothers and sisters? Whenever you come together, each one has a hymn, a teaching, a revelation, a tongue, or an interpretation" (1 Cor 14:26), he put no limits on it; he did not make it gender-specific but addressed it to both men and women. When the church came together, there was an expectation of a whole group of people sharing, male and female, not just two or three at the front, or 'ordained' clergy, it was a whole 'body ministry.' There was no platform, no pulpit, no orders of service. The Body was full of the life of the Spirit. And that life was manifested through the ministry of the various members, both men and women. There was praying, praising, preaching, teaching, words of knowledge, words of wisdom, spiritual songs, hymns, healings and deliverances, the breaking of bread—and women, as well as men, were involved in it all! Some meeting!

These things are a challenge to every generation, as the tendency is always towards professionalism and settling. As time goes by, various structures are established. People don't have the same encounters with the Spirit as their forefathers and mothers. Form takes over, and if we are not careful, fossilisation. Unless. Unless there is a new hunger for God, a new thirst for the realities of the Spirit, and the fresh winds of heaven blow upon us. And so goes the story of revival after

---

[42] William Perkins, *The Art of Prophesying*

revival and the subsequent development of new movements of the Spirit, whether Reformation, Baptist, Methodist, Pentecostal, Charismatic, or Restoration etc.

The challenge in looking at this subject is to lay aside our prejudices and our preconceived ideas and attempt to get at the author's intent regarding the text. That's not easy. I know I have my filters, my lenses through which I have read and interpreted the text, biases which it is not always easy to lay aside, and fears too. My early Christian life was male-oriented in every way, apart from the tearoom. Men led the service; men prayed; men preached; and women cleaned and served the tea. One thing that has always caught my attention is missions. In many settings, it seemed fine for women to go on mission, to be missionary pioneers, brave women, bold women, women of faith, evangelists. For some reason, they could 'teach' overseas but not at home. But even abroad, once things were established, the men would take over.

So far in our exploration of scripture, God's original intention, and the nature of the New Testament church, neither Paul, nor any other writer, appears to have excluded women from any area of service in the life and ministry of the church, so what of the so-called problem passages?

# CHAPTER SIX
## *Exploring the Problem Passages*

I guess some have been longing to get to this chapter if you haven't already jumped ahead to do so. I hope not, as you will have missed my reason for looking at the larger picture first. If you have, I would encourage you to go back and start from the beginning.

So, what about those passages that appear by a plain reading of scripture to exclude women—verses such as 1 Corinthians 11:2-16 and 14:33-36, or 1 Timothy 2:11-15, the "go-to" passages among complementarians—how are we to understand them? In this chapter, we will take a closer look at them along with some others, but first, it would be helpful to make a few comments about how we approach and seek to understand the scriptures.

## *The Plain Reading of Scripture*

At first glance, the plain reading of Scripture seems good and right, but in fact, it may be a superficial or false reading. You may have heard of the old maxim, "When the plain sense makes sense, seek no other sense." It sounds good, right, spiritual, but, and it's a big one, it can lead us in the wrong direction.

We have all no doubt read something someone has written, whether in a book, an email or a text message and thought we had read and understood it correctly, only to discover that we hadn't. Perhaps we read into the text from where "we are standing," or the plain reading turned out to be assumed. Maybe we didn't take into account the context, the grammar, the tone. Maybe we read it from a place of pain and, in doing so, assumed a meaning and reacted—who hasn't done that?

A plain reading of scripture is not then as straightforward as it sounds. For example, John Mark Hicks lists twelve historic interpretations of 1 Timothy 2:12![43] That should give us reason to pause for thought! For example, when Paul writes to Timothy and says, "I do not allow a woman to teach or to have authority over a man," we would need to ask what kind of man? In most countries in the West, it would be anyone over eighteen years of age. But in Jewish culture, it was different. The Torah says thirty, but another milestone was fifty when they were allowed to sit at the gate.[44] In seeking the right understanding, we have to ask how a writer is using a particular word. We also need to know how the context im-

---

[43] John Mark Hicks, "Fourteen Questions About and Eleven Interpretations of 1 Tim 2:12," Online at:
https://johnmarkhicks.com/2021/03/15/fourteen-questions-about-and-eleven-interpretations-of-1-timothy-212

[44] Rabbi Dr. Boruch Leff, "Turning 30,"
http://www.aish.com/ci/s/48917052. html "Dvar Torah, Shabbat Bereishit 5766, (Sermon on Genesis, delivered on a Saturday in Jewish calendar year, 5766)". http://www.neshamah.net/Divrei%20Torah/Bereshit%205766.htm

pacts how that word is to be understood—we can't just grab a dictionary or lexicon and say that's it.

That's why it was good to step back from the negative, or prohibitive, texts regarding women for a moment or two and get the bigger picture, the larger sweep of scripture on the subject. Now, having explored the role and ministry of women throughout the Bible, we can take a look at the passages of scripture that seem to contradict everything we've said so far and, in doing so, start from a "positive affirmation rather than a negative negation."

In doing so, it's right that we follow good principles of Biblical interpretation:

**1. Context is king—always!** If we ignore the context we have a pretext. Context involves not only the chapter, the book, and the Bible as a whole, but also the historical, cultural, and literary context. So what does the context tell us?

**2. Unclear passages, or seemingly contradictory passages, must yield to clear passages.** If the passage that we are looking at is unclear, priority must be given to those that are clear. In the case of women and their involvement in the church, we have already noted that there is an overwhelming "yes" in the larger canon of Scripture. Having said that, there is an argument among complementarians that certain passages in this debate have exegetical precedence. Hence books and papers that start and end with 1 Timothy 2:9-15. Why, and who decides, I'm not sure.

**3. Incidental passages must give way to teaching or instruction passages.** Passages that are not directly related to the subject matter, that may imply certain things, need to give way to those that are deliberately providing teaching and instruction on the subject.

**4. Scripture is interpreted by scripture.** There is more to the Bible than 1 Timothy 2. All scripture, as Paul said, is

"God-breathed and profitable." We can not simply cut and paste what we like.

**5. Check out words.** Discover how a writer uses them. For example, we can't assume that James uses words in the same way as Paul does—to do so pitches Paul against James; or that the writer is using a particular word the way it is in the pagan world.

When all is said and done, we are seeking the author's intended meaning, not our own.

## *Translation and translations*

Before we dig in, it would be good to say a bit about translation and translations, as this has a bigger impact on the subject than you might realise. There are many good, even very good, translations available to us today. We are spoilt by the choices we have; the NKJV, NRSV, NIV, ESV, CSB, MEV, NLT, NASB, etc. and each of us will have our preferences. All of them are reliable and trustworthy. Worth studying. But there is no such thing as a pure translation, that is, one without some measure of interpretation. That might come as a bit of a shock, but there can't be because of who we are. We are not perfect, and therefore we all have a tendency to approach things with some measure of presupposition and bias, however much we may attempt to step back from them. There have been times when I have read or heard things through such filters and refused to go down a particular route of understanding because of such presuppositions and bias. John McKinley, associate professor of theology at Talbot School of Theology, put it this way, in *Bible Translations and Theology (part 2)*:

> "English translation of biblical text unwittingly presents more emphasis on men in a way that the

original authors did not intend for their readers. Readers of some of today's popular translations (ESV, NIV, NASB) hear an unwittingly distorted biblical voice that God speaks primarily to men about men, leaving women to the margin of the passages where females are unavoidably in view (such as narrative accounts with women characters.)"[45]

Having said that, it has to be said that some translations openly acknowledge their intention when going about the task. In our present context, this means that some bible versions have been translated with an acknowledged complementarian bias. If we are not aware of this, we may read them and conclude from what we have read, that scripture is indeed complementarian in its teaching regarding the nature and roles of men and women and their relationship to one another in the home and the church. The English Standard Version, most used by conservative Reformed Christians and churches, appears to fall into this bracket. As it says on the Council for Biblical Manhood and Womanhood website concerning the Literary ESV: "The new ESV takes an unapologetically biblical stance on God's gracious plan regarding the complementary roles of men and women."[46]

In several places, the ESV translators have opted for a complementarian reading. When Paul writes regarding Phoebe, in the eyes of the translators, she is a "servant" of the church and not a "deacon." Junia in Romans 16:7 is noted as

---

[45] John McKinley, Bible Translation & Theology: part 2. Https://www.biola.edu/blogs/good-book-blog/2021/bible-translation-theology-part-2 July 30, 2021

[46] Council for Biblical Manhood and Womanhood, https://cbmw.org/2007/10/08/literary-esv-is-unapologetically-complementarian/

being "well known to the apostles" and not "among them." In 2 Timothy 3:6, the ESV talks about "weak women" rather than "gullible." The translations, "servant," "well known to" and "weak," suit and serve a complementarian agenda.[47] In 1 Cor 11:3, the ESV has, "But I want you to understand that the head of every man is Christ, the head of a **wife** is her **husband**, and the head of Christ is God," (emphasis mine), whereas nearly every other version has "the head of a woman is man…" We'll take a closer look at this passage later on.

In Romans 12:6-8, a section about various aspects of ministry in the church, some versions have up to nine gender-specific references where there are none in the original, and yes, you've got it, they are all male. Interestingly, the ESV doesn't use that many, but where it has used them, it says something. The two times it does are for the gifts of teaching and exhortation. This once again is translating to promote an agenda and is therefore being read into the text. Likewise, in 1 Timothy 3:1-7, there are numerous male pronouns and possessives in some versions that are not there in the Greek. We'll take a closer look at those verses when we come to them, but it's helpful to note them here. My encouragement would be to make use of a range of translations, compare them with one another, and ask with an open mind, why some translators have chosen to translate or add words that differ from others. Did they have an agenda? Is the translation valid?

---

[47] "Bible Translations, Agendas, and Gender Bias" with Allison Barr and Scott McKnight. Podcast: A Pastor, and a Philosopher Walk into a Bar

Richard Burgess

## *Our Hermeneutic*

Aside from the plain reading and the translation of the scriptures, is our hermeneutic, our theory and methodology of interpretation, or our endeavour to discover the author's intended meaning. The evangelical approach has been one of "trust" whereas the feminist approach has been largely through a "hermeneutic of suspicion," a suspicion that the text may not be correct. Not only that, but the text has been overlaid and interpreted "androcentrically"—that is, from a male perspective.

This approach sees the true word of God, as buried under many "man" layers that need to be removed for us to be able to hear what God has to say. It also means that a man can't be trusted to do it because of who he is and his ingrained "blindness" to the truth. While studying for a master's, I had to write an essay as if I were a particular feminist theologian, corresponding with a liberation theologian. It was challenging, but also helpful as I began to question why she would think and write as she did.

To be able to hear, really hear, another's story is vitally important to understanding where they've come from and how their thinking has been shaped. Frequently, it seems as if many, in reaction to their cultural background, swing to the opposite extreme.

The feminist theologian in question had come from a strong, male-dominated part of the church with little if any room for women. She believed that God created woman in his image, equal to man and that there was a place for women in the church. She wanted to investigate this and develop a framework for understanding scripture in this way.

In our response to such an approach, we can end up digging our heels in and developing a hermeneutic that is just as reactive and selective and framed as much by our own social, religious, and cultural experience, rather than an honest, humble hermeneutic that seeks to be true to the fully "God-breathed" Word. Posing questions and wrestling with scripture is the task of every generation, wherever we might find ourselves.

Our hermeneutic then is vitally important. The problem is that women's ministry is frequently assessed through an Old Testament hermeneutic rather than a New Testament one. Ben Witherington, who did his doctoral thesis on women in the New Testament, explains in an article, *Why Arguments against Women in Ministry aren't Biblical*:

> "The problem here is essentially a hermeneutical one. Somewhere along the way about the time when the church became a licit religion under Constantine the OT hermeneutic took over, a hermeneutic which saw churches as temples, the Lord's Supper as a sacrifice, ministers as priests, the Lord's Day as the sabbath, and so on. This did a grave dis-service to the newness of the new covenant and its facets and features, and the net result was an exclusion of women from various ministries, on grounds the writers of the NT would have rejected outright."[48]

## *"Women should be silent" 1 Cor 14:33-36*

An easy place to start is Paul's request for women to remain silent in the churches in 1 Corinthians 14. We already know that earlier in the book (chapter 11), Paul had not prohibited women from taking part in the meetings but affirmed

---

48 Ben Witherington, "Why Arguments against Women in Ministry aren't Biblical,"
https://www.patheos.com/blogs/bibleandculture/2015/06/02/why-arguments-against-women-in-ministry-arent-biblical/ 2015

and encouraged the role of women in both prayer and prophecy. Likewise, through the general encouragement regarding the gifts of the Spirit in chapters 12-14. Therefore, the silence he is talking about is not a broad or absolute silence of exclusion but must be a silence relating to a specific situation.

The context of all that Paul is dealing with here is proper order, or the healthy functioning of the 'body' when it comes together—not church structures. By extracting these verses from both their immediate and larger context, we can make them say something that Paul never intended.

Paul has already said in 1 Cor 14:26, "each one has a hymn, a teaching, a revelation, a tongue, or an interpretation," something clearly addressed to all, both men and women, without reservation. Then at the end of the verse, he says, "Everything is to be done for building up." So, here is Paul's concern for proper order.

The gifts and ministries of the Spirit are good and right, and all may participate in them, but they need to be exercised in a way that is beneficial to all who are gathered. He then applies his thinking to the gift of tongues, which they were using in an unhealthy manner. So much so, that they may even cause outsiders or unbelievers to think "you are out of your minds" (14:23), and so he goes on to say concerning tongues in 14:28 that if there is no one there who can interpret, the person who has the gift should remain silent, or be quiet. It was not a permanent silence. No interpreter, no tongues. About prophesying, he says, "If something has been revealed to another person sitting there, the first prophet should be silent" (14:30). Again, the silence is governed by the context. So by the time we come to verses 33-36, we can see where Paul is going. This is not about silencing women, but managing a particular situation that was causing disruption and confusion in the meetings, thereby impacting their edification and their testimony. It is not teaching, but questions that are the issue being addressed.

In the lecture settings of the day, it was not unusual for students to interrupt speakers with reasonable questions relating to the lecture as they had some knowledge of the subject, but the uneducated were not permitted to do so as it caused disruption. Perhaps it was going over old ground, primary material, rather than taking the subject forward. Maybe you've been in a classroom or lecture theatre when that happened. The lecture was disrupted, taken off course, and you ended up frustrated because you wanted to get on with the subject.

Most women were uneducated and therefore encouraged to learn at home from their husbands, unlike most men, who learned to recite the Law when growing up and therefore would have had a good grounding in the Word. Learning and teaching, if equipped, were not an issue. Eugene Peterson translates the passage, "Wives must not disrupt worship, talking when they should be listening, asking questions that could more appropriately be asked of their husbands at home. Wives have no license to use the time of worship for unwarranted speaking" (I Corinthians 14:34-35, MSG).

## "The man is the head of the woman" 1 Cor 11:2-16

Familiar words, but are we too familiar with them, and in doing so, have we become selective in what we are hearing and therefore believe the text is saying something that it's not? Straight off, we read and hear the word "head," and with it, we encounter the subject of what has been termed "headship," though we should say that Paul doesn't use that term, and the doctrine of "headship" was not on Paul's agenda. Headship is something that has been developed from or read back into the text by later generations who would have a vested interest in a doctrine of headship, or patriarchalism.

The danger in coming to this text or any other is that we home in on a particular word, look up the Greek, and draw our conclusions. First, we need to note the larger context where Paul is encouraging both men and women in their participation in the ministry of the church. Second, we should notice that the focus and force of Paul's discussion is the interdependence that exists between men and women and that all originates in and from God. This must frame how we approach our understanding of the word "head."

There are questions about whether "head" is the best interpretation of the Greek word *kephale*. In these few verses, it is used in two ways: as a literal head and as a metaphor. It has been the subject of much scholarly research, debate, and writing in recent years, which I don't have the space or time to go into here because of its complexity, but here is an outline of various approaches to the text.

**Head as ruler.** When we think in terms of the English word "head," it's easy for us to think of the person at the top, i.e., the headmaster in a school, the boss, or the one who rules and to whom all are answerable. This has been the common or traditional understanding, and the argument for it is strong, an argument largely based on the use of *kephale* in pagan culture.

Pagan culture certainly believed that someone who was the "head" was superior and exercised authority, but that doesn't mean that that is how Paul used it or intended it to be understood. Not only that, it goes in the opposite direction to the teaching of Jesus in the gospels, the new creation, and the nature of the kingdom of God. Jesus confronted such desires and behaviour in his own disciples and taught them that they were not to have or exercise power and authority in the way the world does: "You know that those who are regarded as rulers of the Gentiles lord it over them, and those in high positions act as tyrants over them. But it is not so among you... For even the Son of Man did not come to be served, but to serve, and give his life as a ransom for many" (Mark 10:42-45). The kingdom of God is of a different nature to the kingdoms of this world. It was neither built on nor intended to function according to the fallen principles of this world that have been judged in Christ and are passing away.

Another argument against *kephale* as "head/ruler" is that it creates a problem when we read that the "head of Christ is God." This implies that there is a hierarchy and inequality within the Trinity, something which the early councils of the church rejected as a heresy known as subordinationism (more on this later under The Subordination of the Son). As a result, the term "head" cannot refer to the "ruler" or "one in authority over" in Paul's instruction here.

**Head as the source.** Another way of thinking about "head" that fits with the context but takes us in a different and more helpful direction relates to the head of a river or its source. This seems to fit with what Paul is developing here. Paul explains his use of the word "head" in his discussion of origins (1 Cor 11:8, 11-12), where he defines "head" (Greek: *kephale*) as the "origin" of beings.[49] Therefore, Paul is not setting up a marriage construct for the present, but referring us back to the creation narrative.

---

[49] Grace Ying May, Hyunhye Pokrifka Joe, "Setting the Record Straight, A Response to J I Packer's Position on Women's Ordination." *Priscilla Papers* vol. 11, no. 1 (Winter 1997), 3.

Kenneth Bailey in *Paul Through Mediterranean Eyes*, interprets it like this:

> "The origin of every man is Christ" (i.e. Christ is the agent of God in creation. In 1 Corinthians 8.6 Paul affirms that Jesus Christ is the one "through whom are all things.")
>
> "The origin of woman is man" (i.e. Genesis 2:21-23). Woman [ishah] is "taken out of man [ish]."
>
> "The origin of Christ is God" (i.e., the Christ is "the Messiah" and the origin of the Messiah is God). In the language of later centuries, "The Son proceeds from the Father." Christ comes from God."[50]

Some, though, would suggest that this also undermines the doctrine of the Trinity. It really depends on how we understand the language being used, and as we've said before, language is important. Certainly, this view is not as problematic as seeing *kephale* as head. Following Kenneth Bailey's interpretation, we could use the term "life-source." So the life-source of man is Christ, the life-source of woman is man, and the life-source of the incarnated Christ is God. Taking this approach, when we read that Christ is "the head of the church" in Eph 1:22; 5:23, we understand it not so much in terms of authority but as the life-source of the church without which it cannot exist.

**Head as foundation.** Yet another way is to see *kephale* as a foundational word, which is how it is translated in Matthew

---

[50] Kenneth E. Bailey, *Paul Through Mediterranean Eyes: Cultural Studies in 1 Corinthians* (Downers Grove: InterVarsity Press, 2011). Quoted at https://margmowczko.com/head-kephale-does-not-mean-leader-1-corinthians-11_3/

21:42 and Acts 4:11,12, "The stone that the builders rejected has become the *cornerstone.*" The cornerstone was the foundational and guiding point for the rest of the building. Looking at it this way, each part is seen as an important building block, each contributing and moving towards the whole. This again has some mileage to it.

**Men, women, or husband and wife?** Another question of this passage is, who is Paul referring to? Some versions make it a general reference to men and women, others to husbands and wives. To read it as a general reference to all men and women would mean that all women, married or not, should recognise man as head. Some have gone down that route in the past, but it throws up its own set of problems.

However we approach it, and whichever angle we would prefer to take, we can be sure that rather than developing a hierarchy of relationships, Paul is emphasising the essential unity of men and women in Christ. Man came from Christ, woman from man, Christ from God. So Paul can say, "In the Lord, however, (or nevertheless in the Lord, a reference to the new creation) woman is not independent of man, nor is man independent of woman. For as woman came from man, so also man is born of woman. But everything comes from God." Paul distinguishes between the sexes and then rejects the notion that such a distinction implies a hierarchy of authority and subordination because man is also descended from woman.

## *"Her head uncovered" 1 Cor 11:3-16*

A vast amount has been written and said about these verses regarding head coverings. The chapel I grew up in had this scripture hanging up in the entrance as a reminder to the women of the need to wear a head covering, along with a hat for any woman who had forgotten hers or didn't realise she needed one. For the vast majority, this is no longer an issue—hats disappeared a long time ago. Whatever is involved in this text regarding head coverings, one thing we can be sure of is that Paul was certainly not prohibiting women from taking part in the church meetings when they gathered together.

The context, which is frequently overlooked, is the praying and prophesying of women. Paul was not limiting their gifts or involvement. Rather, his concern was that they function in a way that respected the culture they were in while not compromising or undermining the gospel. That culture no longer exists in much of the world today. Head coverings, for many, have no such cultural meaning. To believe and behave as if they do locks us into the past and undermines the gospel in the present.

What is important to note here is that for mission to be effective, we do need to understand the culture we find ourselves working in and work out how to be a gospel community in that situation. That is something every missionary, every church, has to do, but also something that applies within the varying spheres of life in differing parts of the nations we live in. But that is another subject.

## *"I do not allow" 1 Tim 2:11-15*

This passage is *the* "go-to" passage for complementarians. It stands at the top of the list and is central to their thinking and practice. In it, the complementarian beliefs are affirmed and enshrined in the teaching that from creation, God has intended male authority (headship) and female submission, a consequence of which is that women have no place in teaching or exercising authority where men are concerned. Egalitarians, as you can imagine, have a rather different understanding and take a different approach.

In coming to Timothy, we should remind ourselves that Paul's letter to Timothy is set within the larger framework and context of scripture and what it says regarding the role of women in the life and ministry of the church, and that includes Paul's writings. Many read the rest of scripture through the zoom lens of 1 Timothy 2: 11-15 when this scripture should be read through the wide-angle lens of the rest of scripture.

As we have seen, Paul did not exclude women from ministry. They had just as much right to function according to the gifts God had given them as any man, and women who were gifted and able to teach could do so publicly as well as privately. Secondly, Paul's letter to Timothy is a pastoral letter written to Timothy as Paul's representative at Ephesus. It was not written to the church, and the clear implication is that Timothy knows only too well the situation at Ephesus and exactly what he is talking about, whereas we do not. Not only that, we come at it centuries later, distanced by time, knowledge, and experience. The question then is, why the apparent prohibition? What is going on that necessitates it? Let's take a look at a few of the options and approaches that are out there.

**A specific situation.** As we noted above, 1 Timothy 2:11-15 is a good example of why a plain reading of scripture is not necessarily the right reading of scripture. Especially when we consider that there are twelve historic readings of verse 12 alone.[51] Without an understanding of the problem, we are in danger of drawing the wrong conclusions and proof-texting.

---

51 https://johnmarkhicks.com/2021/03/15/fourteen-questions-about-and-eleven-interpretations-of-1-timothy-212

The fact is, much theological discussion has gone on around the nature of the problem Paul was addressing.[52] Much of Paul's writing is in response to questions and problems that have arisen in the life of the churches. Many commentators on both sides of the present discussion, both complementarian and egalitarian, agree that there is an occasional or temporal nature to the pastoral letters that Paul addresses in writing to Timothy and Titus. In other words, Paul is writing to address a specific situation or situations that have arisen in the church, in a particular place, and not necessarily establishing a blueprint for every church throughout all time and in every place.[53] The challenge of the passage is demonstrated by the number of possible interpretations by complementarians alone—one writer in researching the text has found no less than eight different interpretations by complementarian authors.[54] On such a basis, no one can claim that the meaning of the text is obvious! So what is going on?

**Quietness.** Regarding the question of quietness, "A woman is to learn quietly with full submission…" (1Tim 2:11), we know that this cannot be a reference to absolute silence, as Paul has encouraged and spoken about their participation elsewhere. The quietness Paul speaks of here, then, must be in respect to learning, of having the right attitude towards the one teaching, not too dissimilar to his instruction to the church at Corinth. We also know that Paul had no problem with Priscilla and Aquila, the husband and wife team, teaching and instructing Apollos, and therefore he could not have been opposed to a woman teaching a man. If we understand

---

[52] I am aware that Paul's authorship is debated by some.

[53] Grenz and Kjesbo, *Women in the Church. Ch 4, loc: 1457, 1511.*

[54] Dr Jamin Andreas Hubner, *Patriarchy Rears its Head (Again).*
Online at: scotmcknight.substack.com, May 21, 2021.

that Phoebe was the one who delivered the letter to the church in Rome, we know that, in all likelihood, she was more than just the postwoman delivering it, but would have read it and answered questions about it on behalf of Paul. We also know that Paul affirmed women as his co-workers in the gospel, as ministers. So what is happening here?

Once again, context can help us, and the context here has to do with the proper, orderly, and healthy functioning of the body of Christ. In chapter 2:1, Paul talks about "prayers and intercessions" and in verses 8 and 9, he goes on to deal with how both men and women should go about it, by "lifting holy hands" and dressing "modestly," matters of manner and demeanour, not of office and structure. The problem we face is perhaps not helped when we get to verse 12, when Paul, in most versions, appears to go in a different direction. But does he?

**A temporary injunction.** Aida Spencer, sees Paul here as issuing a temporary injunction, as "slowing down the process," which would ultimately lead to the full and equal participation of women. In other words, he wasn't against women in leadership, but both women and society were not ready yet.[55] Later, in his letters to Timothy, Paul referred to women as idlers, gossips (speakers of foolishness),[56] and busybodies who say things they shouldn't, and what's more, they were doing this from house to house (1 Tim 5:13; 2 Tim 3:6). Women still had much to learn, and learn they could, but there was a way to do that, "quietly and with full submis-

---

[55] Aida Spencer, quoted in "A New Case for Female Elders: An Analytical Reformed-Evangelical Approach." (University of South Africa, 2013). 45.

[56] Fee, *Listening to the Spirit in the Text,* 152 note.

sion" (1 Tim 2:11) — the focus is not on the learning, but on the "manner and mode" in which they do so.[57]

**False teaching.** Another approach is to see Paul as dealing with false teaching, which, according to Gordon Fee, is almost always paid lip-service to by those who believe 1 Timothy was written as a "church manual."[58] Paul starts his letter to Timothy with an urgent call for him to remain in Ephesus because a situation had arisen and needed dealing with. It concerned what he describes as "false doctrine" that involved paying "attention to myths and endless genealogies…" that led to speculation rather than "God's plan, which operates by faith" (1 Tim 1:3,4). He then closes his correspondence in a similar vein with an encouragement to Timothy to "teach and urge these things" and "if anyone teaches false doctrine and does not agree with the sound teaching of our Lord Jesus Christ and with the teaching that promotes godliness, he is conceited and understands nothing" (1 Tim 6:3-4). Rather, he says they crave controversy, enjoy quarrels about words, stir up envy, dissension, slander, evil suspicions, and create friction.

These then are the bookends and give us a clue to the purpose of Paul's writing, which is not simply the correcting of doctrine as an intellectual exercise or providing an instruction manual on how to do church, but rather that it impacts upon everyday life and hinders the gospel. Good, sound doctrine leads to transformed lives, which Paul describes in terms such as "love that comes from a pure heart, a good conscience, and a sincere faith" (1 Tim 1:5), and is demonstrated

---

[57] Quoted in "A New Case for Female Elders: An Analytical Reformed-Evangelical Approach." (University of South Africa, 2013) 232.

[58] Fee, *Listening to the Spirit in the Text*, 148.

by "lifting up holy hands without anger or argument," (1 Tim 2:8), dressing modestly (1 Tim 2:9), exhibiting "good works" (1 Tim 2:10), simply, godliness (1 Tim 4:7,8). Correspondingly, false teaching leads in the other direction and promotes all manner of ungodliness. In all respects, Paul wants them to live saved lives—lives that are a witness to the world in which they live.

In his book *Men and Women in Christ*, Andrew Bartlett, sees the answer as quite straightforward, "In essence the explanation is simple, and it contains no unevidenced speculations... when 1 Timothy was written, there is a crisis in false teaching in Ephesus, as Paul had anticipated would occur."[59] Having excluded two men, Hymenaeus and Alexander, who were possibly leaders or elders in the church, for false teaching (1 Tim 1:20), Timothy was faced with a small number of wealthy widows who had aspirations to eldership. The problem was that they were going from house to house, promoting such things as magic and astrology. Not only that, their manner of dress was costly and provocative, aimed at attracting and seducing men. As the backstory to Paul's letter to Timothy, it provides the context in which it was written and explains the instructions for right conduct in chapter 2:9-15 along with the subsequent instructions for appointing elders.

The context also enables us to understand the movement from 'widows' in 5:11-16 to 'elders' in 5:17-22, something which would otherwise appear abrupt. But, Paul is still on topic and is referring to the wealthy young widows who want to become teaching elders but, at the time of his writing, are not suitable. This leads naturally to Paul's next statement in verse 17, "The elders who are good leaders are to be considered worthy of double honour, especially those who work

---

[59] Andrew Bartlett, *Men and Women in Christ* (London: Inter-Varsity Press, 2019, 2020), Kindle edition, 301.

hard at preaching and teaching..." and on through what he has to say about those who are not behaving as they should in verses 19 and 20 and then to the advice.

**Cultic teaching and behaviour.** Another view relates to the cult of Diana. This is tied to the above but takes it even further. Timothy was at Ephesus at the time of Paul's writing, a place well known for the cult of Diana, or Artemis, a cult that believed that Eve was the originator of Adam and that she was the goddess of life.[60] It taught the superiority of the female and advocated female domination of the male.

Unfortunately, some were into syncretism, the fusion of differing beliefs and practices, and were seeking to propagate them within the church. If that was the case, it certainly makes sense for Paul to say, "Adam was formed first, then Eve…" as a corrective, and, because of these women's strong personalities, temporarily bar them from participating in the ministry of the Word. On this basis, Richard and Catherine Kroeger translate it: "Let the women learn in submission. I do not permit a woman to teach that she is the source for men, but to be quiet (about the fact that all men are born from women.)"

This would appear to make more sense of Paul's reference to "godless myths and old wives tales" (NIV) or "worthless stories that are typical of old women" (NASB), or literally, "old women's tales" in 1 Tim. 4:7, which can seem sexist in our modern context, and indeed out of character for Paul. In their studies, the Kroegers demonstrate that this was a term in contemporary use, referring to old women who were

---

[60] Richard & Catherine Kroeger, "Reading 1 Timothy 2:12 in its Context" https://1timothy2.wordpress.com/ Website condenses the book *"I Suffer Not a Woman: Rethinking 1 Timothy 2:11-15 in Light of Ancient Evidence"* (Grand Rapids, MI: Baker, 1992).

the storytellers in the earth-mother cults. These women were the main propagators of their fertility doctrines and mythology.[61]

Based on the false teaching and cultic teaching approaches to this text, Paul, in writing as he does to Timothy at Ephesus, is not concerned for one moment about maintaining male headship and prohibiting women in general from teaching. Rather, at that moment in time, in that particular place, his concern is the maintenance of 'orthodox' teaching, teaching that has to do with the faith once and for all delivered to the saints, and not a syncretism of differing ideas, cultic or otherwise.

**A Couple.** Another approach is to see it as directed not to the church but to a particular couple, especially a problem wife. In this argument, it is pointed out that earlier in the chapter the references to men and women are in the plural. The men were quarrelling with one another, and the women were dressing to impress. Then in verses 11-15, Paul speaks in the singular of "a woman," and this woman needed to learn and not teach, let alone exercise authority over others.[62]

**Natural law.** Yet another approach is to see what Paul is saying in connection with natural law. This appears to have been the approach of some of the Reformers, who did not read this passage as a blanket prohibition of women but rather interpreted it in the context of "natural law" and "kingdom law" over which God was sovereign. Hence, in this situation, man

---

[61] Richard & Catherine Kroeger, "Reading 1 Timothy 2:12 in its Context."

[62] Margmowczkohttps://margmowczko.com/a-woman-not-all-women-1-timothy-212/

was the head in society—the order preserved by the world and the order preserved by law. For Martin Luther, the idea that women should be submissive was imported from the temporal world. Paul, then, was writing with a sense of expediency. Nevertheless, under the gospel, men and women were equal. This natural law in Luther's mind then applied to the church insofar as the church promotes peace and avoids confusion, but, ultimately, according to Luther, the Christian conscience "knows nothing of the law—but has only Christ before its eyes."[63]

J. G. Brown concluded after doing extensive research on exegeses of the text that, "all prominent Christian theologians before the mid-nineteenth century held something similar to a natural law/two-kingdom view."[64] Patricia Gundry, in her book *Woman be Free*, sums it up well when she says, "The principle set forth seems to be, in accord with the context, that Christians should behave in the public meetings in a respectable manner in accordance with generally accepted standards of propriety."[65]

There is some scriptural weight to this. As Paul says regarding slaves in his first letter to Timothy, they should "regard their own masters as worthy of all respect, so that God's name and his teaching will not be blasphemed" (1 Tim 6:1), and Peter, writing in his letter, encourages his readers to accept the authority of every human institution for the Lord's sake, for "it is God's will that you silence the ignorance of the

---

63 J.G. Brown "A Historian Looks at 1 Tim 2:11-14" (Priscilla Papers, CBE International. 31st July 2012).
https://www.cbeinternational.org/resource/article/priscilla-papers-academic-journal/historian-looks-1-timothy-211-14
64 Brown, "A Historian Looks at 1 Tim 2:11-14"
65 Patricia Gundry, quoted in "A New Case for Female Elders: An Analytical Reformed-Evangelical Approach," 26.

foolish people by doing good. Submit as free people, not using your freedom as a cover-up for evil, but as God's slaves" (1 Peter 2:13-16). The clear implication is that if the early church had gone all out against the norms of the fallen culture of its day, it would have lost its voice, and the cause would have been lost. Rather, the gospel quietly and patiently witnessed to and subverted the culture of the day.

In the intervening years, we have seen a movement away from patriarchalism and the subservient role of women in many cultures around the world. Women are involved in business, education, the sciences, etc., and some nations have had heads of government who were or are women. To quote historian J G Brown, "The authentic traditional interpretation of this passage no longer exists. It is disingenuous for today's hierarchists to claim to be its heirs."[66] Whatever view you feel more disposed to, the fact is that 1 Tim 2:11-15 cannot be said to prohibit women from teaching roles within the church. In fact, if we were to take it as literally as some would suggest, women should not be teaching anyone, children, young people, or even other women. But again, we know that the wider lens of scripture does not say that.

## *"Usurp authority" 1 Tim 2:12 (KJV)*

"But I suffer not a woman to teach, nor to usurp authority over the man, but to be in silence" (KJV). Many modern versions of the Bible have dropped or adapted this phrase so that it reads along the lines "I do not permit/allow a woman to teach or to have authority over a man," yet there seems to be a good reason to retain the older reading. The word Paul uses for authority here *(authentien)* is not the typical one and is

---

[66] Brown, "A Historian Looks at 1 Tim 2:11-14"

only used here in the New Testament. At some point in the twentieth century, interpreters decided to change the word translated "usurp authority" to "exercise authority" or "have authority over." This was a big move away from how it has traditionally been understood, that is, to "take rank and authority away" from the man. George Knight was one of those who made a case for it. We'll say more about that a bit later. For several years, I would have to admit that I was happy to believe the newer versions as they bolstered my complementarian convictions—no more!

Philip Payne in *Men and Women in Christ*, points out that the word *authenteo* is unusual, that Paul uses it nowhere else, and it is not found anywhere else in the Bible. Not only that, it is relatively rare in Greek writings, which begs the question, why would Paul choose such a word and place it in such a letter.[67]

Payne finds connections with astrological language. He notes that Paul uses such language in chapter five to challenge the behaviour of some of the women.[68] The word carries the idea of gaining mastery or dominating. It has origins in the word for murder, and in a related form, means "original." Connected to this are the ideas of "authentic" and "author," meaning to originate. On this basis, Kruger and Kruger argue that the verse could be translated as, "I do not allow a woman to teach or proclaim herself author [or originator] of man..." At the same time, many have dropped the connecting word, which can either be translated as "but" or "and," between verses 11 and 12, and by doing so, make it appear that verse 12 is making an altogether different statement,

---

67 Payne, *Men and Women in Christ*, Kindle version, Why does Paul use the rare word authenteo? 248.

68 Payne, *Men and Women in Christ*. 248.

when in fact Paul is still talking about how a woman may learn.

J David Millar, in an article titled *Asking the Wrong Questions*, notes the complexity of interpretation and how the reader compounds it by asking certain questions that can either guide, limit, or obstruct the process of interpretation. One he notes is regarding role, the other is "When does Paul speak to a specific occasion and when does he speak to all people at all times?" Questions asked and answered by both sides, complementarian and egalitarian. Both, he says, can be helpful, but both can lead us in the wrong direction. The question of role is filled with our notions of it in contrast to what that might have been in the New Testament—think, deacon or minister, for example. With regard to the second, the normative can end up being very selective, i.e., head coverings or braided hair, and who makes the decision? For Millar, then, because all scripture is God-breathed, what we should be looking for is the underlying normative principles, and not seek to dissect Paul's letters in such a way into normative and culturally bound material.[69] On this basis, 1 Tim 2:11-13 are components that contribute to a normative underlying principle, that is, being equipped to teach.

## *"For Adam was formed first then Eve" 1 Tim 2:13*

Many complementarians will say, but Paul then goes on to point them back to the Creation and Fall. Surely that proves the point? Man is the head, woman is to submit. Man is the teacher, woman is the one who is taught. It's a story they will have been familiar with. The danger for us is that we will read it incorrectly and miss the point. In referring to

---

[69] J David Millar, "Asking the Wrong Questions," Priscilla Papers, Vol. 24, No 3, Summer, 2010.

Adam and Eve, the creation story, and the Fall, Paul is calling attention to the fact that Eve was inadequately informed, or taught, and therefore was in a position to be deceived. Adam wasn't. This is about education and the dangers of insufficient instruction, not headship and submission, which are being read back into the text.

God had instructed Adam regarding the tree of the knowledge of good and evil before the creation of Eve, but it appears he had not properly informed Eve. "The LORD God commanded the man, "You are free to eat from any tree of the garden, but you must not eat from the tree of the knowledge of good and evil" (Gen 2:16). Then we read that God said, "It is not good for the man to be alone." So God created woman. Paul says, "Adam was formed first, then Eve. And Adam was not deceived, but the woman was deceived and transgressed" (1 Tim 2:13,14). Rather than this being about women being submissive, weaker or more vulnerable, this is about the fact that Eve was ill-informed, and this set her up to be deceived. Neither is it a comment on the part of Paul that men should do all the teaching and women should listen — again, this is something that is being read back into the text. The ministry of the Word then according to Paul requires, first of all, proper instruction in the Word. The particular woman, or women, at Ephesus, needed instruction.

The only conclusion we can draw then is that Paul is not against women participating in the life and ministry of the church. A unique situation had arisen at Ephesus that needed addressing. The women were not equipped to teach and were usurping/taking authority that wasn't theirs to take or exercise. For this reason, Paul introduces a temporary prohibition until they were sufficiently taught and demonstrated so by their transformed lifestyle. It is for that reason that he writes in the way he does.

## *"He will rule over you" Gen 3:16*

An Old Testament text not referred to by Paul but sometimes cited by complementarians as confirming male authority or rule is Genesis 3:16, "... your desire shall be for your husband, and he shall rule over you." It is variously considered as a woman's sexual desire, with all her desires being subject to her husband; a woman wanting to enslave and control her husband, but he must rule over her (though the text cannot bear the weight of enslaving or controlling); an idolatrous desire on the part of the wife towards her husband; or to rule in general without any overtones of control.

However you choose to interpret it, at face value, this is a description of the consequences of the Fall and its impact on male-female relationships and is not intended to be a reference to God's design or his intention for the permanent state of male-female relations. A breakdown has taken place which has warped the male-female relationship. It was not and is not God's plan. It was part of the curse. But all that changed in Jesus and at the cross, which ushers in a new creation—something alluded to in chapter 3:15. And yes, we do live in the overlap of the now and not yet, but that should not be an excuse to continue a way of life that was not God's intention. We cannot use this text to justify a complementarian view of male-female relationships in the home or the church.

## *"Wives, submit to your husbands" Eph 5:22 (1 Peter 3:1-6)*

This is another text that is commonly used to affirm male authority and female submission, as well as the teaching on "headship," a term that Paul does not use and did not intend to use. The Greek word translated as "head" in verse 22 is *"kephale,"* which is either used literally or metaphorically, as we have already noted regarding its use in 1 Corinthians. As Elaine Storkey, a reformed, British sociologist, is quoted as saying in *A New Case for Female Elders*, "There are always great dangers in building a theology on a metaphor, especially if there is confusion about the meaning of the metaphor." Commenting on its use by complementarians, she says, "Yet, most of these writers see no ambiguity at all... They decide that "head" must mean "authority," construct the notion that "headship" means "male authority," and see it as a general creational mandate," and in doing so, she says, they have "moved from a gentle metaphor to a universal principle!"[70] Something Paul was most emphatically not doing. Gordon Fee makes the observation that "All structures, ours as well as theirs, are predicated altogether on cultural givens. There is simply no biblical structure for the household."[71] Headship then is something that is being read into the passage rather than out of it. It is what's known as eisegesis, not exegesis.

This passage is not about who should lead, who is in authority, or who has the last say, etc., it's about life in the Spirit through mutual submission. Unfortunately, many modern versions place a heading between verses 21 and 22, which distorts the passage. Paul says to all in the church, the brothers and sisters, "Be filled by the Spirit... submitting to one another" (5:18-21). Submission was and is something antithetical to the world and to the Flesh. By nature, we dislike it and

---

[70] Elaine Storkey, quoted in "A New Case for Female Elders: An Analytical Reformed-Evangelical Approach" (University of South Africa, 2013), 72.

[71] Fee, *Listening to the Spirit in the Text*, 71.

fight against it. But it's there in scripture, and there is something beautiful about it, something that contradicts and is counter-cultural to the way of this world. Alan Johnson says in his paper on *A Christian Understanding of Submission* that "mutual submission is a unique practice related to Christ, the Christian community and gospel realities."[72] There is then something to be said for it. Mutual submission means going the way of the cross, of learning to live a cruciform lifestyle, where the way of the Flesh is put to death as we learn to follow the way of the Spirit. And it applies to men and women, to husbands and wives.

What we forget when we read this passage is that female submission was already the norm in a patriarchal society, so why would Paul call upon them to submit? Some have said it was because some of the wives were abusing their newfound freedom. This doesn't seem likely. In some versions, "submit" has been added to verse 22. If we read it, without it, it says, starting at verse 18, "be filled with the Spirit… submitting to one another in the fear of Christ. Wives, to your husbands, as if to the Lord…. Husbands by loving your wives just as Christ loved the church and gave himself up for her" (Eph 5:18-22 — my paraphrase). Reading it without the added "submit" suggests that what follows is a description of what submitting to one another looks like. Both aspects, submission and love, are mutual. The command to love is not only that of husbands but wives, indeed all, whether married or single (Eph 5:1,2; Titus 2:4).

What Paul is calling them to is a radically new kind of relationship where the husband and the wife have a completely different way of relating that involves a mutual submission

---

[72] Alan Johnson, "A Christian Understanding of Submission, A Nonhierarchical-Complimentarian Viewpoint," Priscilla Papers, Fall 2003 17:4

under the Lordship of Christ. It would change the way men thought about their wives and the wives about their husbands. This was not about possession, one being weaker than the other, or a hierarchy of relationships where one is in authority and the other subservient. It is about marriage reflecting something of the love of Christ for the church and the church's love of Christ, something truly sacred. Such a relationship should never be construed in the terms of headship and submission as marked out in the doctrine of headship. The only headship in marriage belongs to Christ, and Christ alone. Men were to love their wives as Christ loved the church and gave himself for her, and wives were to submit to their husbands "in the Lord." Within the bounds of society's structures and expectations at the time, they were to model a new creation way of living as husband and wife, a mildly subversive way that would challenge the norms of the day and point to a better way without actually breaking them.

A similar argument can be made for 1 Peter 3:1-6. Peter's concern, like Paul's, is for the gospel and their witness to the world around them, rather than establishing a universal principle for all people, at all times and in all places. His concern is that Christian wives with unsaved husbands do not abuse their newfound freedom and so discredit the gospel, causing their unsaved husbands to reject Christ.

In saying this, we need to note that authority and submission are not wrong, though the world we live in reacts against such ideas. Indeed, what generation doesn't? Nevertheless, they are part and parcel of life and, in different spheres of life, the problem is when authority becomes twisted into authoritarianism, and submission becomes servitude. That can happen at home, at work, or in the church. May God deliver us from it, and may healing and wholeness follow.

## *The Subordination of the Son*

You might well ask, what does this have to do with our subject? The fact is some have argued that the relationship and role of men and women within the home and the church is based on what we find in the Trinity, and particularly how the Son relates to the Father. This approach speaks of the subordination of the Son of God to the Father from all eternity, and that the will of the Son is subordinate to the will of the Father in all things. More to the point, it says, the Father rules over the Son eternally. In other words, there is a hierarchy within the Trinitarian relations, a hierarchy on which male and female relationships and roles are to be modelled. This has been a key component of the complementarian argument.

Wayne Grudem, the writer of a popular systematic theology, has argued, along with others, that the Father and Son are, "equal in divinity but that the Son has submitted to the Father eternally."[73] On this basis, man and woman are recognised as equal before God, yet have different roles, involving the submission of one, the woman, to the other, the man.

Following a crippling explosion on Apollo 13 in 1970, came the words, "Houston, we have a problem" (or at least the film version's response, in reality, it wasn't quite so stated). The fact is, the teaching of subordination and with it the doctrine of headship, has caused a serious problem that has impeded many a marriage and many a church and continues to do so. And yes, church, "we have a problem," or in the correct words spoken that day, "we've had a problem." At the time they didn't know what had happened, but being alerted to it everyone swung into action to find the problem and resolve it. Likewise today.

---

[73] https://news.sbts.edu/2016/11/18/ets-2016-ware-defines-trinity-view-mohler-urges-conviction-compassion-transgender-issues/

Following much debate in theological settings, the argument has gone against the complementarian position. The debate concluded that the Son was not subordinate from all eternity and that the idea is contrary to both scripture and the historic creeds. Moreover, it was considered a dangerous position to argue from as it posited an inequality within the Trinity. To get an idea of the nature and breadth of the debate, please see the reference below.[74]

So it was in June 2016, that Professor Carl Trueman of Westminster Theological Seminary, a complementarian, wrote these words:

> "Complementarianism as currently constructed would seem to be now in crisis. But this is a crisis of its own making—the direct result of the incorrect historical and theological arguments upon which the foremost advocates of the movement have chosen to build their case and which cannot actually bear the weight being placed upon them."[75]

To back up, in 1977, a book was published in response to the rising challenge of feminism called, *New Testament Teaching on the Role Relationship of Men and Women*, by George Knight 3rd. In the book, Knight rejected the idea of men being superior and women inferior (the prevailing attitude for centuries) and instead formulated a complementarian view based on

---

[74] https://www.booksataglance.com/blog/twenty-sixth-updated-edition-trinity-debate-bibliography/

[75] Carl Trueman, *"Motivated by Feminism? A Response to a Recent Criticism,"* Postcards from Palookaville (blog), Mortification of Spin, Alliance of Confessing Evangelicals, June 7, 2016, http://www.alliancenet.org/mos/postcards-from-palookaville/motivated-by-....

roles. Men and women were equal, but their roles were different. The focus on "role" was new, and was used to affirm the equality of the sexes but explain differences in function and order. A man was to "rule," to have authority, and the woman was to be "submissive" and "obey." This he said was how God set it up in creation and therefore mandated for all times and cultures. He also, for the first time, tied the understanding of a man and woman's relationship to the doctrine of the Trinity, where, according to some, the Son is eternally subordinate to the Father and that this is what Paul was referring to in 1 Corinthians 11:3[76].

Then along came Wayne Grudem and his *Systematic Theology*, which many evangelical and Reformed Charismatic complementarians would use as their primary text. In it, Grudem adopted and popularised Knight's viewpoint. Making the case for a hierarchical Trinity, Grudem maintained equality by making a distinction or differentiation between role and person—though subordinate in role, the Son is not subordinate in person. This was a novel construction that was to have a huge impact on evangelicalism and which the uninformed complementarian took in (something I did).

Kevin Giles points out that before the 1970s, no one ever suggested a differentiation between men and women based on God-given roles and that the use of the word as an interpretive device undermines scriptures "own view that men and women are differentiated by their God-given natures."[77] Today, as noted by Carl Trueman, such complementarianism

---

[76] Kevin Giles, "Complementarian Theology in Crisis." CBE International, https://www.cbeinternational.org/resource/article/complementarian-theology-crisis Oct 24. 2018.

[77] Kevin Giles, "Women in the Church: A Rejoinder to Andreas Kostenberger," *Evangelical Quarterly*, 73:3 (2001), 225-245, 237.

is in crisis as both sides accept that the theological argument regarding the subordination of the Son no longer holds water, and is a faulty basis on which to build the doctrine of the submission of women in the home and the church.

Grenz and Kjesbo quote J. I. Packer following the Colloquium on Women and the Bible (1984) as saying,

> "While it would be inept euphoria to claim that all exegetical questions tackled have now been finally resolved, I think the New Testament papers in particular make it evident that the burden of proof regarding the exclusion of women from the office of teaching and ruling within the congregation now lies on those who maintain the exclusion rather than on those who challenge it."[78]

## *"And Junia" Rom 16:7*

The New Testament speaks about the five-fold ministry of apostle, prophet, evangelist, pastor, and teacher—some see it as fourfold with pastor/teacher being one ministry (Eph 4:11). Whether Paul intended for it to be so closely defined as we have come to understand it is a matter for debate. Again, the list is not gender-specific. In 1 Corinthians 12:28, Paul notes various ministries: apostles, prophets, teachers, miracle workers, those with gifts of healing, helps, leadership, and speaking in tongues. A similar list is found in Romans 12. Sometimes these lists are carved up in a way that Paul didn't intend: into creation gifts, ministry gifts, and spiritual gifts, then sub-divided into gifts of power, gifts of speech and gifts of healing.

Paul was not writing to neatly delineate them and their spheres, but to demonstrate the tremendous variety of God's

---

[78] Grenz and Kjesbo, *Women in the Church.* Kindle loc: page 141.

gifts and that they were all of One. It would therefore seem strange to divide them up as clergy and laity or men and women. At no point does Paul do that—He has referred to men and women in Chapter 11; he could have done so here; but no, the whole chapter on the gifts and ministries of the Spirit is without reference to either male or female roles. All that Paul says is that no one has everything, and that we need them all, and that it is the Spirit who distributes these gifts to the body as he wills.

Some may argue that in these passages, Paul is assuming that we will understand it as men; however, why should we? The answer might well come back that it was a patriarchal culture, and therefore that's how we should read them. Maybe, but on the other hand, Paul proclaims a gospel that doesn't just make the old life better, so we have a better form of patriarchalism. No, he proclaims a gospel that radically transforms it so as to restore God's intention to every sphere of life.

Paul was no male chauvinist, or worse still, misogynist with a massive male ego, as some are inclined to think. A proper study of the scriptures shows that Paul sought to elevate women through his teaching and practice. He was very grateful to God for them and their ministry. They were women of no small character, ability, or gifting. They were women he was proud to count as his co-workers in the gospel. A notable example was Phoebe, who it is generally agreed, took his letter to the church in Rome. That was a huge responsibility. The couriers of those days did not merely pick up a letter or parcel and drop it off like the postman or delivery person, take a photo of it as proof of delivery, and go (it couldn't have been a small thing). The person doing it was chosen based on personal knowledge. They would need to represent the author, so they needed to know him or her, be acquainted with their teachings and be able to articulate them. When they delivered the letter, they would more than likely read it, take questions, answer them, and expand where necessary. Such was Phoebe. Paul also referred to Phoebe as a "succourer" (KJV) or "helper" (NKJV) of many (Rom 16:2).

Paul also refers to Junia, a much-debated character. It would appear the name was originally translated as Junia, but later, around the time of the Middle Ages, became a man's name Junias, though such a name is unknown in antiquity, and there's no supporting evidence for it. Most translators now accept that it was a lady's name, and the debate now runs around the words that describe her, as either "outstanding among the apostles" or "well known to the apostles" (ESV), "outstanding in the view of the apostles" (NASB), "noteworthy in the eyes of the apostles" (CSB). Was she outstanding as an apostle, or outstanding in some other way to the apostles? There's quite a difference!

"Apostle" comes from the Greek word *apostolos*, which means, "envoy, ambassador or a messenger commissioned to carry out the instructions of another." They are "sent ones." The New Testament speaks of Jesus as an apostle sent by God, the twelve apostles who were commissioned by Jesus, and the apostles of the churches. Paul says, "he gave some to be apostles…" Apostolic ministry was to be a continuing gift to the church. It seems strange to suggest, as Schreiner does, that Junia can be a missionary and a church planter but not an apostle![79] As a young person, this was one of the things that fascinated me, women could be on the mission field but relegated to other areas of service at home. They could preach and teach on the mission field but could only "share" a testimony in the church or churches at home.

---

[79] Schreiner, Belleville, Blomberg, and Keener, *Two Views on Women in Ministry*, 258.

In the patristic era, Origen thought that Junia was a woman, and John Chrysostom, though not a supporter of women bishops, held Junia in high regard and considered her to be an apostle: "Indeed to be an apostle at all is a great thing; but even to be amongst those of note; just consider what a great iconium that is… Oh how great is the devotion of this woman, that she should even be counted worthy of the appellation of apostle."[80]

There seems, then, to be no reason for Junia not to be counted as an apostle, and if there could be one female apostle, there no doubt could be others. And if one wants to go down the line of order or priority, Paul says, "God has appointed these in the church: first apostles, second prophets, third teachers…" (1 Cor 12:28), and in writing to the church in Ephesus he said, "The gifts he gave were that some would be apostles, some prophets, some evangelists, some pastors and teachers" (Eph 4:11 NRSV). That would suggest apostles were very influential in the leadership, life, and ministry of the New Testament Church. Please note there is no invisible line through that verse that confines apostolic (and prophetic) ministry to the New Testament era.

Still, some will ask, but what about eldership? Isn't the pastor, or pastor/teacher, an elder? Didn't Paul write to Timothy at Ephesus regarding elders? And isn't it clear that women are excluded? In the next chapter, we'll take a closer look.

---

[80] Grenz and Kjesbo, *Women in the Church.* Kindle Loc: 1069

# CHAPTER SEVEN
## *Exploring Eldership*

What about eldership? Can women, married or single, be elders? That's probably the biggest question for many. Perhaps it's accepted that women can teach, preach, and lead in some areas, i.e., children's work, ladies' ministry, etc., but the role of eldership is the place where the line would be drawn. Some, on the other hand, may be happy for a woman to be an elder or its equivalent, so long as it is not the senior, or lead elder, but remember, there are no Biblical categories for what we may term a senior pastor/elder.

In answer to the question, many will immediately and without hesitation say, "No they can't, Paul says in 1 Tim 3:1-7, that eldership is male only." But, does he? So we turn to our bibles and read and note the frequent male references to "any man," "he," and "his," in just a few verses, and we say, "There you are, look, it's straightforward, obvious, male-only, Paul does not allow it."

Again, I ask, but does he? With all these masculine pronouns and possessives in the first seven verses in most English translations, it would appear cut and dried, with no further argument. But, and it's a big but, the Greek text reads quite differently. All verbs in the Greek are generic, meaning they can be applied to either male or female subjects, and there are no masculine pronouns or possessives. That means that when we read the first verse, we discover that Paul is actually saying, "This is a faithful saying: If someone desires to be an overseer (bishop or pastor), they desire a good work," not "If a man…" If Paul had wanted to say that eldership was male-only, he could have used language that would have expressed exactly that (as many Bible versions have chosen to do), but he didn't. He chose not to. Several versions now translate it as, "whoever," "anyone," or "someone," but unfortunately they revert to the masculine in the next clause, "he desires a noble task." But that's not how it reads. The 2011 NIV translates it as, "Whoever aspires to be an overseer desires a noble task."

To back up for a moment, when we start chapter 3 (remember they weren't there in the original), it can seem as though Paul was changing the topic, veering off in another direction. But stepping back and taking a second look suggests that this is a follow-on from what he has been saying. The conversation and the instruction are continuing. In the previous chapter, he has been talking about "a woman," wanting to function in an authoritative role, but the fact is, she was not equipped and ready to do so. In fact, it would be dangerous for her to do so (in another context, of course, that could be said of some men). So we can read Paul as saying, "it's not out of the question, it's a good thing for anyone, including a woman, to have such a desire to serve in this way, but let me tell you what it looks like. You see, certain qualities are necessary for a leader, for an elder, and it would be good if these qualities were fully demonstrated before giving such space and roles to anyone."

Now, of course, some may argue, "OK, I get the point on the Greek, but surely when Paul goes on to say that that person must be "the husband of one wife," that seals it, and that's why the translators have added the masculine pronouns and possessives." In the Greek, "husband of one wife" is simply a "one-woman man," an idiom or way of speaking. In other words, what we have here is a reference to marital faithfulness, something which would apply to any woman who desired to serve in that way, a "one-man woman." If the phrase were to be taken literally, it raises more questions than answers, and the text presents us with more problems. For example, the reference to children is not singular but plural. Does that mean that no one could be an elder, or lead elder, who wasn't married or didn't have a minimum of at least two children? That would rule out singles and couples without children. We know that in both instances, no one takes it that way. The reference to a "one-woman man" then is not a reference or preference regarding gender, but one of marital faithfulness.

The passage becomes clearer when we read it in a way that truly reflects the Greek. The Common English Bible (2011), for example, renders the Greek into English in a way that recognizes the fact that there are no masculine pronouns or possessives in the text at all, though translators persist in putting them there.

For contrast, here is a traditional translation (I've done an amalgamation so as not to make it version-specific; some versions have fewer pronouns and possessives. I've also deliberately underlined and put them in bold for impact):

"This saying can be trusted: If anyone sets **his** heart on being an overseer, **he** desires something excellent.

An overseer must have a good reputation. **He** must have only one wife, be sober, use good judgment, be respectable, be hospitable, and be able to teach. **He** must not drink excessively or be a violent person, but he must be gentle. **He** must not be quarrelsome or love money. **He** must manage his own family well and **his** children should obey **him** respectfully. (If a **man** doesn't know how to manage **his** own family, how can **he** take care of God's church?) **He** must not be a new Christian, or **he** might become conceited and arrogant and so come under the same condemnation as the devil. **He** must also have a good reputation with those who are not Christians, or **he** might become the victim of disgraceful insults that the devil sets as traps for **him**."

That's a lot of male pronouns and possessives in just a few verses, especially when they are not there. On that basis, it's not surprising that we should draw certain conclusions from it as to male and female roles. The plain reading would seem to make it abundantly clear. So here are the same verses in the Common English Bible:

"This saying is reliable: if anyone has a goal to be a supervisor in the church, they want a good thing. So the church's supervisor must be without fault. They should be faithful to their spouse, sober, modest, and honest. They should show hospitality and be skilled at teaching. They shouldn't be addicted to alcohol or be a bully. Instead, they should be gentle, peaceable, and not greedy. They should manage their own household well—they should see that their children are obedient with complete respect, because if they don't know how to manage their own household, how can they take care of God's church? They shouldn't be new believers so that they won't become proud and fall under the devil's spell. They should also have a good reputation with those outside the church so that they won't be embarrassed and fall into the devil's trap." (1 Tim 3:1-7 CEB).[81]

The Common English Bible also translates what Paul has to say to Titus regarding the appointing of elders in the same way:

"The reason I left you behind in Crete was to organize whatever needs to be done and to appoint elders in each city, as I told you. Elders should be without fault. They should be faithful to their spouse, and have faithful children who can't be accused of self-indulgence or rebelliousness. This is because supervisors should be without fault as God's managers: they shouldn't be stubborn, irritable, addicted to alcohol, a bully, or greedy. Instead, they should show hospitality, love what is good, and be reasonable, ethical, godly, and self-controlled. They must pay attention to the reliable message as it has been taught to them so that they can encourage people with healthy instruction and refute those who speak against it." (Titus 1:5-9 CEB).

Another version that translates it in this way is the Contemporary English Version. If we were to do a plain reading here, we would come to a different conclusion. Some may question the translations of "supervisor" or "spouse," though the constant repetition of masculine pronouns and possessives in other versions would seem to be the more serious problem.

---

[81] Common English Bible, 2011.

Of course, it may be argued that the translators of this version have an egalitarian bias. That I don't know, but spouse fits with the context and tenor of what Paul is saying. On this basis, we cannot use this passage to say that Paul is prohibiting women from functioning in the role of eldership or of lead elder, and whether male or female, the qualifications required are appropriate for both.

Now someone might come back and say, "Just a moment, Paul doesn't mention any women elders by name." Maybe, but anyone who does so is on a "sticky wicket," to borrow a cricketing term, as he rarely mentions any men by name either. Outside of Paul, only Peter and John are identified as elders (1 Peter 5:1; 2 John 1:1 and 3 John 1:1). It's possible that Priscilla was an elder. In his letter to Timothy, Priscilla seems to have been a leader alongside her husband in the house church at Ephesus and later in Rome. It should also be noted that in his letter to Timothy, Paul uses both the masculine and feminine forms of the Greek word (*presbyteros* and *presbyteroi*).

Some complementarians think that there is a difference between a pastor and an elder, the first being a gift, the second an "office."[82] One is received, the other is an appointment. Every elder would be a pastor, but not every pastor would be an elder. This seems to be an attempt on the part of some complementarians at some kind of accommodation of women's ministry. In scripture, the words "pastor," "elder," and "overseer" are used interchangeably (1 Peter 5:1,2).

Frequently, it's said that there is no evidence of female elders in the early church, so women should not be elders in

---

[82] Sam Storms, "Is it Biblically Permissible for a Woman to be Called a 'Pastor'?" https://www.samstorms.com/enjoying-god-blog/post/is-it-biblically-permissible-for-a-woman-to-be-called-a--pastor-/ 04.05.2022.

the church today. That may have been the case, but as more research is being done and documents are discovered, that idea is being challenged. To quote Charles Stelding,

"To date, historians have found evidence for almost a dozen female presbyters dating from the second to the fifth century. There were woman elders at least until the 4th century, because the Council of Laodicea (AD 363-364) forbade any more presbytides being ordained (Canon 11). Atto, bishop of Vercelli (10th century), summarizes that, before the Council of Laodicea "female presbyters" "assumed the office of preaching, leading and teaching." They "presided over the churches." The Acts of Philip (4-5th century) assumes male and female presbyters. Within that community, women as well as men served at all levels. One list mentions "presbytides" (female elders or priests) alongside "presbyters" (male elders or priests). In some instances, "presbyter" refers to an administrative duty, such as the administration of burial places. In other cases, women performed liturgical functions, a practice attacked by Gelasius I at the end of the fifth century."[83]

In their book, *Ordained Women in the Early Church, A Documentary History*, Madigan and Osiek go so far as to say, "What can be said with certainty is that the claim that women have never functioned as presbyters in the "orthodox" church is simply untrue."[84] Among those they reference in their work

---

[83] Charles Stelding, Women Presbyters/Elders in the NT and the Ancient Church quoted on https://margmowczko.com/women-elders-new-testament/

[84] Kevin Madigan and Carolyn Osiek, eds., *Ordained Women in the Early Church, A Documentary History* (Baltimore, MD: John Hopkins

as elders are, Ammion, Artemidora, Epiktō, Kalē, Leta, Martia, Flavia Vitalia, and Guilia Runa.

As more work is being done, it is becoming increasingly apparent that as the church became more and more institutionalised, the names of women were edited from the record. One such case concerns Theodora. Outside the chapel of St. Zeno in the Church of St. Praxida, a fourth-century church in Rome, there is a mosaic depicting four women: two saints, Mary, and a fourth woman with the inscription *Theodora Episcopa*. Episcopa is the feminine form of "bishop." In the image, Theodora is seen to be wearing the headdress of an unmarried woman, and around her head is a square halo, which signifies a living person. Everything in the mosaic points to the fact that she was a bishop. What is of particular interest is that at some point in time, someone has tried to remove or cover over the 'ra' at the end of Theodora, thereby attempting to make it a man's name, and hide the historical reality that a woman had been a bishop in the church.

From the start in the Garden of Eden, it was never God's intention for man to be alone. Neither was it God's intention that man alone should "rule." Man was not complete. God made him a helper who was different to him but equal to him. Together they were equipped for the task of stewarding creation to the glory of God. Together, equal. Not one above the other. God has gifted men in a variety of ways. God has also gifted women. When there are only men sitting at the table we are going to be missing something. I wonder how many male elders have gone back home to their wives and talked about some aspect of church life that they have been discussing only for their wives to say "didn't you consider

---

University Press, 2005, 2011), Kindle edition: end of first chapter.

this or that?" Women have an array of gifting. We need one another. They tend to have a greater spiritual depth than men, their relational abilities tend to exceed those of men. They are great at nurture and tend to be high in emotional intelligence and good at integrative thinking.

As we have seen throughout our study, in the "age of the out-poured Spirit," women could exercise the various gifts and ministries of the Spirit in exactly the same way as the men. And as we have seen, Paul does not hold back in commending women as apostles and prophets, which in Paul's mind and teaching are first and second-order gifts in the church, above that of teachers (1 Cor 12:28). For Paul, calling, gifting, and learning are the operative words, not inflexible structures that stifle the life and ministry of the Spirit. Ultimately, authority is in the calling, gifting, and ministry of the Word, not in the 'office' or the person, whether they are male or female.

Eldership in the early church was a team ministry, Titus was left by Paul in Crete to appoint elders in every town, not an elder (Titus 1:5). Whether someone led the team is debatable. We may deem it right that someone does, but it is a team of equals. There will be different gifts and abilities, strengths and weaknesses. As each function according to their gifts, so they are given the space and responsibility needed. In such a team, there will be an interplay of leadership. And as we have seen, there seems to be no reason to bar women from teaching in a mixed congregation or entering into leadership roles, including those of eldership and senior leader.

In the next chapter, we are going to do a grand sweep over two thousand years of church history and encounter some amazing women of God. Women who will challenge and inspire.

# CHAPTER EIGHT
## *Exploring Church History*

Sadly, the focus in church history has frequently been on men, to the neglect of women. Reading some stories of revival, those times when there were fresh moves of the Spirit, women were very much involved, but as time went by and structures were put in place, men assumed authority and the women were excluded, and, it appears, written out of the story. Scholar Laura Swan, in her book *The Forgotten Desert Mothers*, sums up the situation:

> "Women's history has often been relegated to the shadow world: felt but not seen. Many of our Church fathers became prominent because of women. Many of these fathers were educated and supported by strong women, and some are even credited with founding movements that were actually begun by the women in their lives."[85]

---

[85] Swan, L. *The Forgotten Desert Mothers: Sayings, Lives, and Stories of Early Christian Women* (Mahwah, NJ: Paulist Press), 2001.

Sadly, the medieval church even considered women to be dangerous temptresses who should be avoided at all costs.

In this chapter, we are going to take some time to explore the role of women throughout church history. In doing so, we'll see how God has used them to do some incredible things in the life and mission of the church right down through the centuries, and across a variety of Christian traditions, many in difficult and trying circumstances.

As I have looked afresh at some of the women I knew and discovered others that I had never heard about before, I have been stirred afresh at how God has not only called and equipped men to fulfil his purposes, but women also. That he desires to see them released to fulfil their callings and roles in today's church. In doing so the church will benefit beyond measure.

These can only be brief introductions, although some have grown longer than my original intentions! I would encourage you to go and explore their stories in greater detail. You can do a lot by searching the internet, and there are also individual and collected biographies of many of them.

**Thecla** (first century AD). Though questions have been raised as to her existence, she was spoken of in the affirmative by Gregory of Nazianzus and Basil of Caesarea. Thecla is reputed to have become a Christian through hearing the apostle Paul and became a devoted follower of Christ. She had a teaching centre and a hospital at Seleucia, which remained in operation for a thousand years. Thecla appears to have been a truly heroic character who endured all manner of suffering for the sake of Christ, and though her story seems to have been embellished, causing many to dismiss it, modern scholars believe that she actually existed.[86]

**Ammia** (first mentioned around 160 AD). Ammia prophesied in Philadelphia during the New Testament times, and it is possible she knew the daughters of Philip who are mentioned in the book of Acts. She was received throughout Asia Minor with reverence and was listed as a prophet by the church historian Eusebius.

**Alce/Alke** (late first-second century AD). A woman of high status, who was possibly a patron of the church at Smyrna, and appears to have exercised quite an influential ministry within it. Ignatius twice refers to Alce as "dear to him", once in a letter to the church at Smyrna and the other in a letter to Polycarp, the bishop of Smyrna. He also greeted Tavia and her household, much like Paul does.

**Macrina the Younger** (328-380 AD) healed, prophesied, and actively spread the faith. Her faith and devotion to God inspired the work and lives of her more well-known younger brothers, Saint Basil the Great (329-379 AD) and Saint Gregory of Nyssa (335-395 AD). Gregory wrote of her to a friend, "In this case it was a woman who provided us with our subject; if indeed she should be styled woman for I do not know whether it is fitting to designate her by her sex, who so surpassed her sex." He also spoke of "her noble career."[87]

**Saint Paula** (347-404 AD). Saint Paula, the sister of Augustine, was a close associate of Jerome and encouraged and inspired him to translate the Bible from Hebrew and Greek into Latin. She also proofread and edited it before it was published. This translation, known as the Vulgate, would be used

---

86 https://christianhistoryinstitute.org/magazine/article/women-in-the-early-church.

87 Medieval Sourcebook: Gregory of Nyssa (c.335-d.c.395): Life of Macrina.

as the church's authoritative scripture for the next 1,500 years. She travelled widely with Jerome and was involved in establishing a religious centre in Bethlehem.

**Marcella** (325-410 AD). Marcella grew up in a Christian family. After the death of her young husband, Marcella vowed to remain single and began a Christian community in her palatial home for women who had taken a similar vow. They prayed and studied the scriptures. Marcella both taught and instructed in the scriptures and theology, and could challenge any heresy. Jerome stayed in her home for three years while translating the scriptures, and with her knowledge of Greek and Hebrew, she was able to offer him critiques of his work. Because of her scholarship, he was quite happy to refer church elders to her for the resolution of a hermeneutical problem. The church father Athanasius was another notable who stayed in her home from 338 to 340 AD.[88]

**Catherine of Siena** (1347-1380). In her late teens, Catherine learned to read and became familiar with the early church fathers, such as Gregory the Great and Augustine. Some would term her a mystic due to the accounts of her spiritual experiences, but she was also considered to be a great theologian. Not only was Catherine intensely spiritual and someone who exercised her mind deeply in the Word, but she was also very practical and involved in ministry to the poor, the sick, and the imprisoned of Siena.

**Genevieve** (419-512 AD). In 451 AD, she led a prayer marathon that is believed to have saved Paris from Attila's Huns. Genevieve was a holy woman who functioned as an ecclesiastical leader. The ministry and role she fulfilled were every bit that of a bishop without the title, though she wasn't

---

[88] Marg Mowezko, Marcella of Rome: Academic and Ascetic, https://margmowczko.com/marcella-of-rome-academic-ascetic-and-almsgiver/ accessed 04.11.2021.

ordained and didn't perform the sacraments. She was responsible for taking care of Paris during a famine. She travelled through areas she oversaw administratively, exercised power and authority, and was received by local dignitaries with all the honours that were traditionally reserved for male leaders, all things expected of a bishop at that time.

**Brigit of Kildare** (451-525 AD). Much of Brigit's life is surrounded by myth and folklore. Whether she was raised as a Christian or converted is debated by some, but early in life she was taken up with the preaching of Saint Patrick, and devoted herself to a religious life, much to the dislike of her father. According to legend, she was sold with her mother to a Druid family, which she later led to the Lord. She is credited with the founding and building of a double monastery for men and women in Kildare around 470AD, which became an acclaimed centre of education, pilgrimage, worship, and hospitality, with priests and people coming from far and near. Brigit was a compassionate woman, a friend of the poor and a peacemaker, and was well known for her generous hospitality. Scholars tell us that she presided over the local church and, in many respects, exercised a role similar to that of a bishop, a role to which she was ordained, though she rejected the ecclesiastical title and didn't perform the sacraments. Some struggle to accept that Brigit was a bishop and try to argue it away, yet Patrick was not made or ordained a bishop by anyone but seems to have pronounced himself to be one, and they have no trouble with that!

**Marie Dentiere** (1495–1561). Marie Dentiere was born in Tournai (modern Belgium) to a wealthy family and entered an Augustinian nunnery in 1508 (the same order as that of Martin Luther), where she received a good education, which would have included extensive knowledge of the Scriptures. In 1521, at the age of 26, Marie was elected Abbess. Impacted and captivated by the teaching of the Reformation and its emphasis on salvation by grace, through faith, in Christ alone, she converted to the Reformation and fled from Tournai to Strasbourg in 1524 to escape the resulting persecution. While there, she met and married a young priest, Simon Robert, and both she and her husband tirelessly preached in favour of the Reformation. She was the first woman theologian of the Genevan Reformation. Through her study of the scriptures, Marie was passionate about women being treated in the same way as men and having a larger role in the life and ministry of the Church, something which angered the Genevan authorities.

Dentière knew Hebrew and Latin and helped her husband translate the scriptures into the vernacular. Three documents are attributed to her, a French grammar; a history of the Reformation as it happened in Geneva; and a letter to the Queen of Navarre, entitled *A Most Beneficial Letter*, her most famous and controversial work, a letter with over two hundred biblical references! In it, she makes a robust biblical defence of Reformed theology, refutes the idea common at the time that women were the source of evil, and makes an impassioned attack on the Catholic Church. Not only did she attack the Catholic Church, but she also defended the right of women to be theologians and teachers, saying, "For what God has given you and revealed to us women, no more than men should we hide it and bury it in the earth. And even though we are not permitted to preach in public congregations and churches, we are not forbidden to write and admonish one another in all charity."[89] The letter caused an uproar, the printer was arrested, and most of the copies were destroyed. Nevertheless, Marie's question to Marguerite of

---

[89] Epistle to Marguerite de Navarre, 53.

Navarre remained: "Do we have two Gospels, one for men and the other for women?" Marie Dentiere was hugely influential and is the only woman named on the Reformation Wall in Geneva, a monument that honours people, events, and documents of the Protestant Reformation. Other notable women of the Reformation include **Marguerite de Navarre** (1492-1549), **Argula von Grumbach** (1492-c.1554), and **Katherine (Schutz) Zell** (German: 1497–1562).

**Katherine Parr** (1512-1548). Katherine was the only wife of the English king, Henry VIII, who wasn't divorced or beheaded. She was born into a family with royal connections and became a widow as a teenager in 1528. She remarried in 1534 to John Latimer, a baron, who introduced her to life at the Royal Court. In 1543, Lord Latimer died, and in the same year, Katherine Howard, wife of Henry VIII, was executed, and Henry set his sights on Katherine Parr, who was now engaged to Thomas Seymour. The King sent Seymour to Europe and married Katherine in a private service on July 12th, 1543. As a young girl, she is said to have told her mother, "My hands are ordained to touch crowns and sceptres, not spindles and needles." Considering that a woman of Katherine's rank hardly ever attained royal status, was this a divine revelation, a prophecy? It certainly seems to have been something that meant a lot to her and perhaps helped her on her journey.

It's not known when Katherine came to faith or how, though she does seem to have been influenced by the Queen of Navarre, Marguerite, who was a godly woman. Following her marriage to Henry, she engaged the services of Protestant tutors for Prince Edward, Henry's son, and appointed a man who was sympathetic to the Reformation to be her chaplain. These were the early days of the Reformation, and being a supporter was not easy as it was not popular or widely supported. Katherine though was undeterred and appears to have been both strong and bold in her faith, and her desire to see it progress. In 1544, she came into close contact with Archbishop Thomas Cranmer, who had been appointed as an adviser when Henry made her Regent while he was away at war.

The subject of religion was a daily aspect of the royal couple's conversation. Katherine encouraged Henry to move away from Rome, pressed him for greater reform of the church, and championed the idea of using English in worship. Katherine's boldness and eagerness weren't wholly welcomed in the Royal Court, and some of Henry's courtiers who were less favourable to the Reformation tried to find a way of curtailing her influence on the King, thereby slowing or stalling the Reformation. Thankfully they were not successful.

Katherine was a lifelong learner and was fluent in French, Latin, and Italian. She also learnt Spanish after she became queen. Katherine was also an author and wrote at a time when it was not popular for women to do so. Among her writings are *Prayers and Meditations*, a devotional work and the first to be authored by an English woman under her own name; *Psalms or Prayers*, a translation of Psalms from Latin into English done anonymously; and *Lamentation of a Sinner*, a personal confession and expression of her faith. In them, we discover a truly spiritual woman. A woman who trusted in Christ as her only hope. A woman who had a deep knowledge of the scriptures, coupled with a passion and dedication to following Christ and making him known. She may have been bold, but she was also winsome in seeking to win others to Christ and the cause of the Reformation.

One cannot tell or measure the full impact of Katherine's influence on the advance of the Reformation. Her contribution to the sphere of education was such that she persuaded the king to approve the founding of Trinity College, Cambridge, in 1546. As a result of modern research, some now believe that Katherine may have had some involvement in the Book of Common Prayer, the official Anglican prayer book, particularly in its prayer for the King.[90]

**Dorothy Hazzard** (1590?-d. 1674). Little is known about Dorothy. After the death of her husband, who was a grocer, she continued to manage the shop in Bristol. She was a supporter of the Separatist movement and was the target of persecution. She remarried in the 1630s to a Puritan preacher by the name of Matthew Hazzard. Matthew became the minister of Christ Church with St Ewen. Following a personal struggle regarding her religious beliefs, she split from the Church of England and joined the Separatists. Dorothy gathered around herself several like-minded friends who were not happy with the established church, seeing its political control and the use of a prayer book as contrary to scripture. The gathering was established as a church in 1640 and, by 1643, had 160 members. It was known as Broadmead Baptist Church, the first Baptist Church in Bristol.

In 1643, when Bristol was besieged by the King, Dorothy was involved in leading a group of women to defend Bristol by blocking one of the gates during the English Civil War. This became the subject of a mural in Bristol's Old Council House.

**Elizabeth Attaway** (1645?). Elizabeth was renowned as a 'tub preacher.' Every Tuesday afternoon she taught the scriptures and exhorted everyone at the General Baptist Church in

---

[90] https://www.evangelicalmagazine.com/article/katherine-parr/ https://www.factinate.com/people/43-little-known-facts-catherine-parr-last-wife-henry-viii/ https://carleton.ca/fass/2016/07/surprising-history-katherine-parrs-prayer-henry-viii/

Bell Alley in London, drawing up to a thousand people. This drew widespread disapproval from the civic and church authorities. Thomas Edwards, a Presbyterian, who has been described as a professional heresy hunter, cites her in his encyclopedia of heresies published in 1646 called Gangraena denouncing secretaries.[91] He had no sympathy for women preachers.

**Margaret Askew Fell** (1614-1702). Margaret was married to George Fox and was one of the co-founders of the Quakers. Their marriage, in modern terms, was what would be described today as egalitarian. Margaret was a woman of high social station, deep spirituality, and strong convictions. She possessed a fire in her belly, a brilliant intellect, and the rhetoric of Luther. Margaret was known as one of the Valiant Sixty early preachers and missionaries and became affectionately known as the Mother of Quakerism. One of the books she wrote was called, *Women's Speaking Justified, Proved and Allowed of by the Scriptures, All Such as Speak by the Spirit and Power of the Lord Jesus And How Women Were the First That Preached the Tidings of the Resurrection of Jesus, and Were Sent by Christ's Own Command Before He Ascended to the Father (John 20:17)*, in which she unpacks passages from Genesis through Revelation that "promote women in ministry and the equality of the sexes in the power and authority of the Spirit." Fell's writings on women in the church, her unofficial teaching, and refusal to swear an oath to the king led to periods of imprisonment.

**Susanna Wesley** (1669-1742). Susanna grew up in a Puritan home with an emphasis on an ordered timetable for the

---

[91] Ruth Goldbourne, "A Short History of Baptist Women in Ministry," www.baptist.org.uk.
Curtis W. Freeman, "Visionary Women Among the Early Baptists," Baptist Historical Society, 2-5. Divinity.duke.edu

spiritual life and the following of regular exercises in Christian obedience as they strove toward perfection. This was to have a lasting impact on her and shaped her approach to life, marriage and the family. At the age of 19, she married Samuel Wesley, an Anglican minister, and they went on to have nineteen children, nine of whom died in infancy. Two of the children we know well, John and Charles, the founders of Methodism, yet her influence was such that historians believe that their success had much to do with their mother, and so she is fondly known as the mother of Methodism.

Susanna was a woman of the Word and prayer. Though she had a large family, she always found the time to pray, sitting in her favourite chair with her apron over her head as a sign to all of what she was doing, and not to be disturbed. She taught her children, giving time to each one. She would gather people around her kitchen table and teach them from the scriptures, and when her husband was out of town, she was the one who kept the parish going. The informal Bible study she conducted after church on a Sunday saw up to two hundred people in attendance. She was also responsible for planting the idea of allowing lay people to serve as local preachers in John Wesley's mind. She may not have had a title or held an office in the church, but she exercised a mighty ministry both in her own family and beyond.

**Selina Hastings, Countess of Huntingdon** (1707-1791). Selina counted John and Charles Wesley and George Whitefield among her friends. She was a woman of power and influence and did not hesitate to use it for the good of revival. She opened many doors, including opportunities for them to preach to the aristocracy and to gain financial backing for their work. Selina devoted herself, her time, and her influence to God, and she also gave her incredible fortune to further the work of the gospel. She took every opportunity to speak to everyone she had contact with about revival and witnessed to it, especially among the nobility.

**Jarena Lee** (1783-1864). In 1819, Lee became the first African-American woman authorized to preach in the African Methodist Episcopal Church. Lee became a travelling preacher, going from one place to another on foot. She faced much opposition due to both her race and gender. In a year, she is said to have travelled, two thousand three hundred and twenty-five miles, and preached one hundred and seventy-eight sermons!

**Unknown women preachers of the Second Great Awakening,** (1790-1845). In the early 1800s, during what has become known as the Second Great Awakening, more than one hundred women were known to have travelled the country as itinerant preachers, many of them unknown today, holding meetings in barns, and schools, or outside in fields. Though there was concern that they would be sentimental in their preaching, they turned out to be fiery preachers of the gospel, not afraid to press its warnings and claims upon those who were listening. Excluded from ministry in the traditional denominations and churches of the day, such women flourished among the new and radical revival movements of the Freewill Baptists, Christian Connection, Methodists, and African Methodists.[92]

**Catherine Booth** (1829-1890). Catherine had a strict evangelical upbringing and attended Wesleyan Methodist classes. She was influenced by the writings of John Wesley and Charles Finney, the American evangelist. In 1855, Catherine married William Booth, and together they were the founders of the Salvation Army. Catherine believed that women could

---

[92] Catherine E. Brekus, "Female Preaching in Early Nineteenth-Century America," (The Centre for Christian Ethics, Baylor University, 2009). 20.

preach, and William, along with many others, didn't. This only served to sharpen her determination. On one occasion, Catherine wrote a rebuttal to a local pastor who demeaned women's spiritual understanding. In it, she argued that nurture, not nature, was to blame, and so she set out to change the status of women in the church through speaking and self-publishing. In 1859, Catherine wrote a pamphlet entitled, *Female Ministry; or, Woman's right to preach the Gospel*, in defence of Phoebe Palmer, a female American preacher.

The year 1860 saw Catherine start preaching, and when William heard her, he changed his mind! Her preaching was dynamic and effective, and she saw many come to faith in Christ. Though she was also committed and worked hard to see social reforms, for many, her lasting legacy would be the change in attitudes towards women in ministry. This led to the Salvation Army publishing a statement in its Orders and Regulations regarding the equality and value of women's ministry.

**Phoebe Palmer** (1807-1874). Phoebe was a famous evangelist and writer. She and her sister began holding ecumenical women's prayer meetings, which multiplied into similar groups around the country. Palmer also began to organise and preach at camp meetings, where approximately 25,000 people were converted to Christianity.

**Antoinette Brown** (1825-1921) became the first ordained Congregationalist woman minister in 1853.

**Fanny Crosby** (1820-1915). Fanny was completely blind yet able to write more than 9,000 hymns, many of which are well known, the most famous being, *Blessed Assurance Jesus is Mine*, a hymn which recounted her personal testimony. She had an amazing memory and committed large portions of Scripture to memory. In 1843, she joined the faculty of the New York Institute for the Blind and taught history and rhetoric for fifteen years. She also had a compassionate heart and cared for the dregs in society.

**Susannah Spurgeon** (1832–1892). Susannah was the wife of the well-known preacher Charles Spurgeon and had a passion to provide poor ministers with good theological resources to aid them in their ministry. She also gave of her own money and set up a book fund to provide free books, which she continued to do for the rest of her life.

**Charlotte 'Lottie' Moon** (1840-1912). Missionary to China. Lottie was one of the first unmarried women to be sent by the Southern Baptist Convention Foreign Mission Board. She spent her entire 40-year career in northern China, where she not only taught Chinese children but was also an effective evangelist of Chinese women and a church planter. Moon waged a slow but relentless campaign in her denomination on behalf of women missionaries who she felt were underrated. She desired that they should have the freedom to minister and have an equal voice in mission proceedings. At the age of 45, she gave up teaching to concentrate fully on evangelising the interior of China. Moon said, "Could a Christian woman possibly desire higher honour than to be permitted to go from house to house and tell of a Saviour to those who have never heard his name? We could not conceive a life which would more thoroughly satisfy the mind and heart of a true follower of the Lord Jesus."

**Maria Woodworth-Etter** (1844-1924). In 1885, Maria started preaching and praying for the sick. Her healing meetings drew large crowds, and she eventually purchased an 8,000-seat tent. Maria had a great burden to see women released into ministry. She was pivotal in founding the Assemblies of God in 1914, and, in 1918, founded what is today Lakeview Church in Indianapolis.

**Mary Slessor** (1848-1915). Known as "Everybody's Mother," Mary was a missionary to Nigeria. An evangelist and teacher, she was one of the first to be concerned about and battle the social injustices that she encountered, and one of the first single missionary women to make a nationwide impact.

**Lilias Trotter** (1853-1928). Missionary to Algeria, who ends up overseeing the missionary work there. By 1920, the work had grown to thirty full-time workers and fifteen preaching stations.

**Kate Bushnell** (1855-1946). Kate studied classics and medicine and joined the Methodist Women's Foreign Missionary Society as a medical missionary to China. After three years, she returned to the United States and became a pioneering anti-trafficking activist, first in the United States, and then around the globe. On her travels, she frequently encountered respectable Christian men abusing their wives, and searching for a reason, concluded, "The crime was in the fruit of theology."

The problem she discovered lay in the Christian teaching of the subservience of women to men; the doctrine of authority and submission. A scholar of Hebrew and Greek, Bushnell went on to study the scriptures in their original languages and historical context. In doing so, she discovered insights sometimes obscured by Bible translators and concluded there was an interpretive bias going on. Kate went on to write *God's Word to Women*, published in 1921, expounding the value and role of women in the church and home. In challenging the issues of the day, she was no liberal or feminist. Throughout her life, she was known for denouncing the evils of modernism and believed the Bible to be everything that it claimed to be: "inspired, infallible, and inviolable."

**Evangeline Corey Booth** (1865-1950). Evangeline was the daughter of William and Catherine Booth, founders of the Salvation Army. She started preaching at the age of 15 and two years later held her first leadership post. Evangeline led the Salvation Army for 30 years before becoming the first General of the International Salvation Army. Evangeline was dedicated to her Lord and believed in living her faith out to the full. One of the things she said was, "It is not how many years we live, but rather what we do with them." She had a gift for solving problems and became the Army's troubleshooter, going into varying situations, whether it was persecution, troubles in a local branch or at an international level. She also wrote several hymns, the most well-known being *The World for God*.

**Amy Carmichael** (1867-1951). Amy was a prolific writer, writing some 35 books. She spent 55 years on the mission field in India and never returned home for a furlough. She founded the Dohnavur Fellowship, a ministry that helped rescue thousands of children who had been dedicated to temple gods and goddesses and suffered horrendous abuse.[93]

**Evelyn (Evie) Brand** (1879-1974). Evie Brand grew up in a fashionable, Strict Baptist home in London. She dedicated her life to winning the people of India for Christ. Despite being a widow, retired, and afflicted with infirmities, Evie travelled from village to village, evangelising on all five mountain ranges known as the Mountains of Death.[94]

---

[93] GFA Missions, Amy Carmichael,
https://gfamissions.org/pages/learn-and-promote/detail/3/27/
[94]
https://www.christianity.com/church/church-history/timeline/1901-2000/evelyn-granny-brand-11630789.html
https://gfamissions.org/pages/learn-and-promote/detail/3/23

**Henrietta Mears** (1890-1963). Henrietta was the Director of Christian Education at First Presbyterian Church of Hollywood. When she took on the job, there was already a thriving Sunday School program in the church, with over 450 children in attendance. Within two years of her arrival, the classes had exploded to over 4,000 students. She produced her own materials, which resulted in a worldwide publishing ministry now known as Gospel Light Publications. Henrietta was also influential in many men and women going into the ministry.

**Amiee Semple McPherson** (1890-1944). Aimee was originally a missionary in China, but after the death of her husband, and finding herself as a single mum, she returned to the United States. There she started a ministry as a travelling evangelist and went on to found Angelus Temple in Los Angeles. In the first seven years, the church attracted 40 million visitors and became the spiritual home to thousands. Her preaching was dramatic and engaging, lasting for an hour to an hour and a half, and was accompanied by many miraculous healings. During the Great Depression, the church fed 1.5 million people. The ministry would eventually grow to become the International Church of the Foursquare Gospel.

**Corrie Ten Boom** (1892–1983). Corrie was imprisoned by the Germans when her family were arrested for involvement with the resistance, by hiding Jews. While she was in the prison camp, Corrie would conduct Bible studies in Barracks 28, a place that became known as "the crazy place, where they hope." Corrie survived the Holocaust, and her story and Christian witness resulted in a prolific writing and speaking ministry. She had the privilege of taking the gospel to some sixty countries before she died.

**Gladys Aylward** (1902-1970). Brought up in a Christian home, Gladys, was determined, "by hook or by crook" to become an actress—until God intervened. With no mission board willing to support her because she was considered to be inexperienced and not educated enough for missionary work, and having very little money, Gladys responded to the call of God to take the gospel to China.[95]

Gladys decided to go by train and worked and saved for her ticket. It was a hazardous journey that would take her through Manchuria, where there was fighting and no guarantee of getting through. Not only that, but the country and culture were alien to her, and it was caught up in the Sino-Japanese War. But, time and time again, she experienced God's intervention in impossible situations, proving that when God calls, indeed, all things are possible.

Her life and ministry would go on to have a huge impact. She is most well known through the film, *The Inn of the Sixth Happiness*, which was loosely based on her life and how she led more than 100 children to safety following the invasion of Japanese forces. Gladys became affectionately known as the "Little Woman" or "Virtuous One."

**Women of the Welsh Revival** (1904-1905). Rather like the Second Great Awakening in the United States, there were many women involved in the Welsh Revival, but little is heard of them. Much is known and heard about Evan Roberts, but there were several women who were used by God before and during the revival. Two of them were Pamela Morgan and Rosina Davis. **Pamela Morgan** (1836-1940), who became known as Mother Shepherd, came to Christ through the Christian Mission, what would become known as the Salvation Army. Pamela soon became known as the "Hallelujah Washer Woman" and was soon engaged in mission activity, sharing her testimony around London. In 1878, she was sent by William Booth to Aberdare in Wales, where she preached

---

[95] Gladys Aylward, *Gladys Aylward: The Little Woman*, (Chicago, IL: Moody Publishers, 1974). Kindle version, location 39.

the gospel with great courage and tenacity, standing in the open-air declaring the love of God and calling people to repentance and faith. Her ministry, in many ways, was a forerunner to the Welsh Revival.[96] **Rosina Davis**, (1863-1949), aged just 14, left home to join a Salvation Army mission in Maesteg. By 1881, she was conducting preaching tours. In 1900, she held a mission service in Llangollen, Denbighshire. Davies was a free church evangelist during the 1904–1905 Welsh Revival, appointed by the Union of Welsh Independents in 1904. Early in 1904, she held missions in Rhosllannerchrugog, and one mission during the autumn of 1904 resulted in two hours of weeping and worship. From 1930 to 1931, she conducted a preaching tour of the USA and Canada.[97]

**Kathryn Kuhlman** (1907-1976). Kathryn was born into a Christian home. Her father was a Baptist, her mother a Methodist, and an excellent Bible teacher. Kathryn committed her life to Christ at the age of 14. After graduation from school, she travelled with her sister and her husband, an itinerant evangelist, on evangelistic trips over the summer holiday, where she would give her testimony. She went on to work with them for five years. After she parted company with them, Kathryn, who was both eager and ambitious to preach the gospel, went on with her pianist Helen Gulliford to conduct revival campaigns in Baptist churches lasting two to six weeks. Eventually, they went on to establish the Denver Revival Tabernacle, which held 2,000 people.

Following a disastrous marriage and divorce that led to the end of her ministry in Denver, Kathryn moved to Pittsburgh and started again. There, she established a radio ministry as well as an influential preaching and healing ministry

---

[96] http://daibach-welldigger.blogspot.com/2016/02/william-booth-wales-2-pamela-shepherd.html

[97] https://peoplepill.com/people/rosina-davies

based in Carnegie Hall, where she held packed-to-capacity meetings until 1971. These meetings reached thousands of people, with many travelling large distances to hear her and to be healed, some testifying to healing whilst on the journey. A notable aspect of her ministry was the words of knowledge that she would have that would release healing into people's lives. From the 1940s to the 1970s, Kathryn travelled the world holding healing crusades. Her ministry also created a bridge between the Pentecostal/charismatic ministry and the historic denominations. Two books she wrote, among others, *I Believe in Miracles* and *God Can Do It Again*, spread the message of God's miracle-working power. Despite all the healings that took place under her ministry, Kathryn never claimed to be a "healer"—she always pointed people to Jesus, who was the healer.

Though she saw many healed, her greatest burden was for lost souls. Speaking of that burden, she said, "I can only tell you that with my conversion, there came this terrific burden for souls. When you think of Kathryn Kuhlman, think only of someone who loves your soul, not someone who is trying to build something—only for the kingdom of God, that's all—souls, souls, souls! Remember! I gave my life for the sole vision of lost souls. And with my conversion, there came this terrific burden for lost souls."[98]

**Sabina Wurmbrand,** Co-Founder of the Voice of the Martyrs, (1913-2000). Many will have heard of Sabina's husband Richard, but Sabina was actively involved in ministry alongside her husband as together they proclaimed the gospel in Communist Romania, running what was a very effective 'underground' ministry. From 1946-1947, she organised Chris-

---

98

https://www.christianlifeministries.com.au/people-of-faith/kathryn-kuhlman/

tian camps for religious leaders of all denominations in Romania and conducted street meetings with gatherings of up to 5,000 people. Sabina actively spoke to churches, groups, and conferences for 32 years after the founding of Voice of the Martyrs and accompanied her husband to testify at Congressional hearings on religious persecution.

**Fuchsia Pickett** (1918-2004). Fuchsia Pickett came to Christ through a Presbyterian friend, was educated at John Wesley College, and was ordained as a Methodist minister. A lifelong student of the Word, she earned three doctorates in theology and a doctor of divinity degree. After becoming seriously ill in 1958, she resigned from her pastorate. On April 12th, 1959, she was carried to a Pentecostal Holiness church, believing it was her last, but God prompted her to go forward for prayer, and she was completely healed and baptised in the Holy Spirit. Her life and ministry were transformed. She ministered as a conference speaker and teacher, where she saw the power of God at work. In 1966, she became head of the Bible department, Academic Dean and Director of a large Bible College in Texas. In 1971, she founded Fountain Gate Ministries with her second husband, Leroy, who she married after the death of her first husband, George. Fountain Gate included an interdenominational church, a Bible college, a Christian Academy, and a daily radio and weekly TV ministry. In 1988, she resigned as pastor of the church, sensing the call of God to go to the body of Christ at large, with a particular emphasis on ministry to pastors and leaders. Fuchsia was also an adjunct professor at Beacon Theological Seminary and in demand as a regular conference speaker. She was the author of more than 10 books and placed a great emphasis on living a crucified life.

**Helen Rosevere** (1925-2016). Helen was a medical missionary in the Congo. When she ultimately returned from

Africa, she had a worldwide ministry of speaking and writing.

**Jackie Pullinger** (1944-). Jackie got on a ship, praying that God would guide her as to where she should get off. That place was Hong Kong, where she became a missionary in the Walled City of Kowloon. The Walled City was known as a lawless slum full of opium dens, pornographic film theatres, and triad gangs who profited from crime and prostitution. She witnessed people of all walks of life, from criminals and gang leaders to prostitutes and drug addicts, come to know Christ as their Saviour and be transformed by his grace. Many were set free from drug addiction, especially dependence on heroin, by praying in tongues. She founded the St. Stephens Society, which continues to serve Hong Kong's poorest. Her story is documented in the book *Chasing the Dragon*, and in a BBC documentary.

**Joni Eareckson-Tada** (1949-). Many will know through the books and subsequent films of the tragic accident that left Joni paralysed from the neck down and the darkness that followed. While in occupational therapy, she learned how to paint with a brush between her teeth and went on to become an accomplished artist. She has written over forty books and recorded several musical albums. From her experiences grew a ministry to accelerate Christian ministry in the disabled community. She founded Joni and Friends in 1979 to provide Christ-centered programs to families with disabled children, as well as training for churches. Joni is a speaker at conferences and an international advocate for people with disabilities.

In this brief overview, an overview that has grown larger the more I researched and studied, we see many women of God, who had notable lives and ministries and left an amazing legacy. Thank God for every one of them and the courage, strength, and faith they had, sometimes against all odds. The last chapter draws our exploration of the role of women in the church to a close with some final thoughts.

# CHAPTER NINE
## *Final Thoughts*

Wow! Some journey. Have you managed to stay with me? For me, it has been a long journey. Not rushed, but considered. Even as I come to the close of it, I have a degree of caution, even reticence, that what I have written will be misconstrued, that I will be accused of giving in to culture, of not holding to a high view of the Word. Like many others, on both sides of the argument, I believe in the fully "God-breathed" word, otherwise known as the plenary (full) inspiration of scripture and my desire is to honour and glorify God by being true to his Word in belief and practice. I understand and respect those who differ. As Paul says, "Everything that is not from faith is sin" (Rom 14:23).

The conclusion I have come to is that scripture puts no restrictions on the role and ministry of women and that they should be encouraged and released into all that God has called and equipped them for. And that, by seeing and enabling women to be all that they can be, will strengthen and enhance church leadership, ministry, and mission. In the world at large, many of those barriers have come down; women run businesses, have been prime ministers, are police chiefs, etc. It's time they did in the church. Not because of feminism, liberalism, or changing culture—though taking the Reformers view a change in culture would be an acceptable reason—but because Scripture, the "God-breathed" word, calls us to it and history testifies to it. In doing so, we cannot be halfhearted about it. To do so will only add to the problem. To affirm the involvement of women but overlook or leave them to one side in preference to a man is not the answer. It will only add to the frustration of those women who feel equally called and gifted. The promise of equality must be lived up to. Opportunities must be truly equal.

Some of those who know me and know my thinking will say to me, "So now you're an egalitarian…" I've never liked labels. They can be misunderstood, misconstrued, used against you, etc., or they can be treated as tribal, identity-affirming markers, "so you are one of us, you're on our side." For that reason, I'm reluctant to call myself an out-and-out egalitarian. Not because I have my doubts, but because labels divide rather than unite, which is the way of this fallen world, and also because in coming to the conclusions I have, truth is never a wholly one-sided thing.

The danger of a full-on egalitarianism would be to say that there are no distinctions, yet, as we have noted scripture doesn't go that far. There are gender distinctions, whether we like it or not. God has made us male and female. We are not the same. We do bring different things to the table. We do truly complement one another and need one another, but the moment we say that God has established a hierarchy of relationship between men and women, we go beyond scripture and undermine that.

Again, all are equal in standing and status before God, but, all are not equally gifted, either men or women. Indeed, the nature of life is such that there must be, in some measure, an inequality of gifting for us to need one another. If we were all equal in our gifting, we would not need one another. Full stop! But that is not how God set things up in the Garden. God made Adam and Eve equal, but unequal. Equal in status, but in need of each other.

There is an old joke that says, "If God had made woman first, he would not have needed to make man." That is just not true. We need one another. God designed it that way. We complement that which is lacking. And as every marriage is different because each couple are unique personalities in what they bring to the covenant of marriage, each couple must ultimately work out what marriage looks like for themselves. Likewise, in our endeavours as God's covenant people. We live by the Spirit, not the letter or the formula. All that it takes for a marriage to be a good marriage of two equals will be required in seeking the full participation of women in the life, ministry, and leadership of the church. A full recognition of equality in person-hood, of gifting and ability, listening and learning, wisdom, effort, faith, grace, energy, and opportunity.

Christ has come and brought about a new creation. The old markers are gone. The dividing lines have been obliterated. He has given us his Spirit, pouring him out indiscriminately on both male and female alike, gifting and enabling both in the life, ministry and mission of the church. The church will be far better equipped by recognising that and releasing and enabling women to be who God calls them to be across the whole life of the church.

When Dallas Willard was asked to write a chapter for the book *How I Changed My Mind about Women in Leadership*, he declined because he said he had always believed that women could be leaders in the church. Instead of writing a chapter, he agreed to write the foreword, and in it, this is what he said:

> "All through my young life (growing up in Baptist churches in Missouri) those who had taught me most "at church" were women. Actually, I knew that, in many cases, there would have been no church at all if it hadn't been for women; and beyond church, life in my environment was mainly anchored in strong and intelligent women who—often with little or nothing in the way of "credentials"—simply stood for what was good and right and directed others in the way of Christ."[99]

He went on to speak of women who would preach if the need required, though the official pastors were men, and how they could do very well at "bringing the message." As Dallas grew older, he concluded that it was a "very weak hermeneutic" that used certain passages of scripture to deprive women of opportunities to lead and minister and was saddened "at how much hurt and harm can be imposed through warping the Gospel and its ministry into cultural legalism in the name of God."

The hermeneutic, as we have seen, is based on a few passages of scripture in relation to the whole and read through a specific lens; it is also a hermeneutic that is more closely tied to Old Testament thinking and practice than to New Testament thinking and practice. Willard goes on to say that the terms of women's ministry are determined by obligation rather than rights or equality, therefore, a woman should be

---

[99] Alan F. Johnson, Ed. *How I Changed my Mind about Women in Leadership* (Grand Rapids, MI: Zondervan Academic, 2010).

able to fulfil everything that God calls, equips, and enables her to do.

As we come to the end of our journey exploring the role of women in the life and ministry of the church, we cannot remain neutral. It demands a response for the sake of women, the church, and the gospel.

# *Bibliography*

Barr, Beth Allison. "The Myth of Biblical Womanhood, A Perspective from Medieval Africa." *Christians for Biblical Equality International*, 24th October 2018.
Bartlett, Andrew. *Men and Women in Christ*. London: InterVarsity Press, 2020.
Belleville, Linda L., Craig L. Blomberg, and Craig S. Keener. *Two Views on Women in Ministry*. Grand Rapids, MI: Zondervan, 2005.
Bird, Michael F. "Some Parts of Evangelicalism Do Not Need to be Deconstructed… They Need to be Destroyed." Online at: https://michaelfbird.substack.com/p/some-parts-of-evangelicalism-do-not?utm_source=url Accessed 25.11.2021.
Boroditsky, Lera. "How Does Language Shape the Way We Think?" https://edge.org, 6.11.09.
Boyd, Gregory A. *Inspired Imperfection: How the Bible's*

*Problems Enhance its Divine Authority,* Minneapolis, MN: Fortress Press, 2020.

Brekus, Catherine E. "Female Preaching in Early Nineteenth-Century America," *The Center for Christian Ethics, Baylor University*, 2009.

Brown, J G. "A Historian Looks at 1 Timothy 2:11-14." The Priscilla Papers, CBE International, https://www.cbeinternational.org/resource/article/priscilla-papers-academic-journal/historian-looks-1-timothy-211-14 31st July 2012.

Cole, Kadi. *Developing Female Leaders.* Nashville, TN: Thomas Nelson, 2019.

Denison, Jim. "What should the Role of Women be in the Church." Online at: https://www.denisonforum.org/resource/faith-questions/what-should-be-the-role-of-women-in-church, October 25. 2019.

Dicks, John. *Hearing Her Voice.* Grand Rapids, MI: Zondervan, 2012/14.

Dixon, Roger. "The Theological Importance of the Term "Father" for God," Online at https://www.biblicalmissiology.org June 15, 2020.

Fee, Gordon. *Listening to the Spirit in the Text.* Grand Rapids, MI: Wm B Eerdmans, 2000.

Freeman, Curtis W. "Visionary Women Among the Early Baptists," Baptist Historical Society, https://divinity.duke.edu/sites/divinity.duke.edu/files/documents/faculty-freeman/visionary-women-among-early-baptists.pdf

Giles, Kevin. "Complementarian Theology in Crisis." *Christians for Biblical Equality International,* online at: https://www.cbeinternational.org/resource/article/complementarian-theology-crisis Oct 24. 2018.

____ *The Headship of Men and the Abuse of Women.* Eugene, Or: Cascade Books, Wipf and Stock, 2020.

____ "The Genesis of Equality, Part 1." *Priscilla Papers,* Vol 28, No 4, 2014.

____ "Women in the Church: A Rejoinder to Andreas Kostenberger," *Evangelical Quarterly,* 73:3, 2001.

Goldbourne, Ruth. "A Short History of Baptist Women in Ministry," www.baptist.org.uk.

Grenz, Stanley J., and Denise Muir Kjesbo. *Women in the Church: A Biblical Theology of Women in Ministry.* Downers Grove, IL: InterVarsity Press, 1995.

Grudem, Wayne. *Evangelical Feminism, A New Path to Liberalism?* Wheaton, IL: Crossway, 2006.

Gundry, Patricia. Quoted in "A New Case for Female Elders: An Analytical Reformed-Evangelical Approach." *University of South Africa,* 2013.

Hicks, John Mark. "Fourteen Questions About and Eleven Interpretations of 1 Tim 2:12." Online at: https://johnmarkhicks.com/2021/03/15/fourteen-questions-about-and-eleven-interpretations-of-1-timothy-212

Hubner, Dr Jamin Andreas. "Patriarchy Rears its Head (Again)." Online https://scotmcknight.substack.com, May 21, 2021.

Johnson, Alan F. Ed. *How I Changed my Mind about Women in Leadership.* Grand Rapids, MI: Zondervan Academic, 2010.

Johnson, Alan. "A Christian Understanding of Submission - A Nonhierarchical-Complimentarian Viewpoint," Priscilla Papers, Fall 2003, 17:4

Kroeger, Richard & Catherine Clark. *I Suffer Not a Woman.* Grand Rapids, MI: Baker Academic, 1992, E-book 2014.

Kroeger, Catherine. "Women in the Early Church."

https://christianhistoryinstitute.org/magazine/article/women-in-the-early-church

Leff, Rabbi Dr Boruch, "Turning 30," http://www.aish.com/ci/s/48917052.html

Lloyd-Jones, D. M., Ian H. Murray, *John Knox and the Reformation.* Edinburgh: Banner of Truth Trust, 2018.

Lockyer, Herbert. https://www.biblegateway.com/resources/all-women-bible/Eve

Madigan, Kevin and Carolyn Osiek, eds., *Ordained Women in the Early Church, A Documentary History.* Baltimore, MD: John Hopkins University Press, 2011. Kindle edition.

May, Grace Ying, Hyunhye Pokrifka Joe, "Setting the Record Straight, A Response to J I Packer's Position on Women's Ordination." *Priscilla Papers,* vol. 11, no. 1. Winter 1997.

McKinley, John. "Bible Translation & Theology: part 2." Https://www.biola.edu/blogs/good-book-blog/2021/bible-translation-theology-part-2. July 30, 2021.

McKnight, Scot. *Reading Romans Backwards: A Gospel in Search of Peace in the Midst of the Empire*. London: SCM Press, 2019.

_____ "Elders, Deacons or Bishops?" https://scotmcknight.substack.com/p/elders-deacons-or-bishops?utm_source=url

Millar, J David. "Asking the Wrong Questions." *Priscilla Papers,* Vol. 24, No 3, Summer 2010.

_____ "What Can We Say About Phoebe." *Priscilla Papers*, Vol 25, No 2, Spring 2011.

Millar, Rachel Green. *Beyond Authority and Submission.* Phillipsburg, NJ: P & R Publishing, 2019. Kindle Edition.

Mowczko, Marg. "Ben Witherington on Jesus and Women," https://margmowczko.com/ben-witherington-on-jesus-and-women

\_\_\_\_\_ "A Woman not all Women, 1 Tim 2:12" https://margmowczko.com/a-woman-not-all-women-1-timothy-212

\_\_\_\_\_ "Marcella of Rome: Academic or Ascetic." https://margmowczko.com/marcella-of-rome-academic-ascetic-and-almsgiver Accessed 04.11.2021

Nyssa, Gregory of. *Medieval Sourcebook: Gregory of Nyssa (c.335-d.c.395): Life of Macrina.* Trans. by W.K. Lowther Clarke, London: SPCK, 1916. Online at Fordham University, New York.
https://sourcebooks.fordham.edu/basis/macrina.asp

Payne, Philip B. *Man and Woman, One in Christ, An Exegetical and Theological Study of Paul's Letters.* Grand Rapids, MI: Zondervan, 2015. EPUB

\_\_\_\_\_ "Is It True That In The NT No Women, Only Men, Are Identified By Name As Elders, Overseers, Or Pastors, And That Consequently Women Must Not Be Elders, Overseers, Or Pastors?" Online at: https://www.pbpayne.com/is-it-true-that-in-the-nt-no-women-only-men-are-identified-by-name-as-elders-overseers-or-pastors-and-that-consequently-women-must-not-be-elders-overseers-or-pastors/

\_\_\_\_\_ "The Bible Teaches the Equal Standing of Man and Woman." *Priscilla Papers*, Vol 29, No 1, Winter 2015.

Perkins, William. *The Art of Prophesying.* Digital Puritan Press, n.d.

Reeves, Michael. *The Good God.* Crown Hill, Milton Keynes: Paternoster, 2012. Kindle Edition.

Ryrie, Charles C. *The Role of Women in the Church.* Nashville, TN: B & H Publishing, 1958, 2011. Kindle Edition.

Schlimm, Matthew Richard. *This Strange and Sacred Scripture: Wrestling with the Old Testament and Its Oddities.* Grand Rapids, MI: Baker Academic, 2015.

Schreiner, T. Linda L. Belleville, Craig L. Blomberg, and Craig S. Keener, *Two Views on Women in Ministry,* Grand Rapids, MI: Zondervan, 2005.

Soloveichik, Meir. "Queen Esther, a Hero for Our Time - A paradox of Jewish fragility and heroism." *New York Times.* March 8, 2020. Online at: https://www.nytimes.com/2020/03/08/opinion/queen-esther-purim.html

Spencer, Aida. Quoted in "A New Case for Female Elders: An Analytical Reformed-Evangelical Approach." University of South Africa, 2013.

Stelding, Charles. "Women Presbyters/Elders in the NT and the Ancient Church" quoted at https://margmowczko.com/women-elders-new-testament

Storms, Sam. "Is it Biblically Permissible for a Woman to be Called a 'Pastor'?" https://www.samstorms.com/enjoying-god-blog/post/is-it-biblically-permissible-for-a-woman-to-be-called-a--pastor accessed, 04.05.2022

Swan, L. *The Forgotten Desert Mothers: Sayings, Lives, and Stories of Early Christian Women*. Mahwah, NJ: Paulist Press, 2001.

Trueman, Carl. "Motivated by Feminism? A Response to a Recent Criticism," *Postcards from Palookaville (blog), Mortification of Spin, Alliance of Confessing Evangelicals.* June 14, 2016. Online at: https://www.reformation21.org/mos/postcards-from-palookaville/motivated-by-feminism-a-response-to-a-recent-criticism#.W8TfuHtKiUm

Witherington, Ben. "Why Arguments against Women in Ministry aren't Biblical," https://www.patheos.com/blogs/bibleandculture/2015/06/02/why-arguments-against-women-in-ministry-arent-biblical

**Websites**
Counsel for Biblical Equality (Egalitarian):
https://www.cbeinternational.org/
Counsel for Biblical Manhood and Womanhood
(Complementarian): https://cbmw.org/
Junia Project https://juniaproject.com/
Women in the Church:
https://christianhistoryinstitute.org/magazine/article/women-in-the-early-church

**Two books to help in creating abuse free communities:**
*Created to Thrive: Cultivating Abuse Free Faith Communities.* Edited by Elizabeth Beyer. CBE International 2021.
*A Church Called Tov: Forming a Goodness Culture that Resists Abuses of Power and Promotes Healing.* Scott McKnight and Laura Barringer. Carol Stream, IL: Tyndale Momentum, 2020.

**Video**
Ben Witherington III, "Jesus and Women."
https://vimeo.com/14172103

## About the Author

Richard is married to Pam, and they live in Ashford, Kent. They have three children, one daughter-in-law and three grandchildren. He has studied at the Wales Evangelical School of Theology (now Union) and Westminster Theological Centre. He has been involved in most aspects of church life and ministry, including church leadership, and presently serves on the leadership team at his local church. His ministry has taken him to Romania, Kenya, and the Democratic Republic of Congo, as well as to local churches. Richard has also written, *Living the Saved Life*, a devotional study of the book of James, and blogs at richardburgess.org. You can also find him on Twitter @ richardburgess2. He would love to hear any feedback and may be contacted at richardburgess113@gmail.com

Printed in Great Britain
by Amazon